GUNS
OF THE
NORTH-EAST

GUNS
OF THE
NORTH-EAST
COASTAL DEFENCES FROM THE TYNE TO THE HUMBER

Joe Foster

Pen & Sword
MILITARY

First published in Great Britain in 2004 by
PEN & SWORD MILITARY
an imprint of
Pen & Sword Books Limited
47 Church Street
Barnsley
South Yorkshire
S70 2AS

Copyright © Joe Foster, 2004

ISBN: 1 84415 0887

The right of Joe Foster to be identified as
Author of this Work has been asserted by him in accordance
with the Copyright, Designs and Patents Act 1988.

A CIP catalogue record for this book
is available from the British Library

Typeset in 9pt Palatino by Pen & Sword Books Limited

Printed and bound in England by
CPI UK

Pen & Sword Books Ltd incorporates the Imprints of Pen & Sword Aviation,
Pen & Sword Maritime, Pen & Sword Military, Wharncliffe Local history, Pen
& Sword Select, Pen & Sword Military Classics and Leo Cooper.

For a complete list of Pen & Sword titles please contact:
PEN & SWORD BOOKS LIMITED
47 Church Street, Barnsley, South Yorkshire, S70 2AS, England
email: enquiries@pen-and-sword.co.uk • website: www.pen-and-sword.co.uk

Contents

Introduction   *6*

Abbreviations   *6*

Acknowledgements   *7*

Chapter 1. History   *9*

    Victorian Muzzle Loading Batteries
    Breech Loading Batteries
    Preparing for War
    The First World War
    Between the Wars
    The Second World War
    The Final Years

Chapter 2. Coast Artillery   *43*

    Muzzle Loading Guns
    Breech Loading Guns
    Hitting the Target

Chapter 3. Gunners   *73*

    Victorian Regulars Militia and Volunteers
    Royal Garrison Artillery
    The Second World War: A Gunner Remembers

Chapter 4. The Bombardment of Hartlepool   *95*

Chapter 5. Gazetteer   *131*

    Tyne Defences
    Hartlepool and Tees Defences
    Humber Defences

Bibliography   *169*

Index   *174*

Introduction

Britain's shores were protected by batteries of artillery from the days of Henry VIII until shortly after the Second World War. In times of crisis they were highly valued. In times of peace they were often left to decay, the guns rotting and their caretakers falling into old age. Only very rarely did they fire a shot in anger. Eclipsed by events elsewhere their remains are largely ignored and their story all but forgotten.

This book deals with the batteries along the North-East coast from Victorian times to 1956, a period of rapid technological change which affected all aspects of life. Our story starts with old-fashioned cannons and ends with guns capable of hitting targets over the horizon and out of sight. It also tells of the one and only time that British mainland batteries ever fought enemy battleships.

It is for the reader to judge their effectiveness as a deterrent. The only serious threat came during the First World War and, although the German Navy was not put off by the guns at Hartlepool, it is telling that they did not attempt to attack more attractive targets at Hull and Newcastle. Perhaps standing offshore was one thing, but passing batteries to enter an estuary or river mouth was quite a different matter.

Abbreviations

AA	anti-aircraft
BL	breech loading
BCP	battery command post
BOP	battery observation post
CASL	coast artillery search light
CD/AA	coast defence anti-aircraft
CHL	Chain Home Low
DCRO	Durham County Record Office
DEL	defence electric light
DLI	Durham Light Infantry
DRF	depression rangefinder
HP	hydro pneumatic
LDV	Local Defence Volunteers
NAA	National Artillery Association
PAD	passive air defence
PF	position finder
pr	pounder (weight of ammunition)
QF	quick firing
RA	Royal Artillery
RE	Royal Engineers
RGA	Royal Garrison Artillery
RML	rifled muzzle loading

Acknowledgements

Coast defence is a relatively unploughed field and this book could not have been written without the assistance of a large number of people. Given the lack of standard texts on the subject there is much room for omissions and mistakes in this book - on my head let them fall!

Particular mention must go to Alan Rudd, an independent researcher, and Ian Stevenson of the Palmerston Forts Society who provided much information, answered numerous impertinent questions, proof read, etc. Also from the Palmerston Forts Society was David Moore who helped tease out a number of particularly difficult questions, particularly with regard to aiming the guns. Incidentally, a number of the gun drawings are derivatives of those held by the society.

Special thanks go to Len Stockill who provided many reminiscences of his time at the Heugh Battery, some of which are published here. Also thanks to John and Brian, his sons, who enabled a meeting with Len and a particularly memorable visit to the battery.

Other people who have helped generously are Norman Litchfield for information and pictures of the Volunteers and Militia, Ray and Amanda Westlake for helping track down obscure texts, Brian Rushworth of Fort Paull for interesting snippets regarding life in the Victorian Battery, Julian Lowerson and Rob Shaw with whom much groundwork was done in the 1970s, also Nigel Evans for checking a number of details.

Public records have been a particularly important source and thanks go to David Butler and staff of Durham County Records Office and the Regimental Association of the Durham Light Infantry for their kind permission to reproduce a number of photographs. Also thank you to Liz Williams of the Northumberland Archives and the staff of the Public Record Office.

The Heugh Battery Gun Trust provided the enthusiasm and commitment that encouraged me to turn a rather obscure hobby into a book, particularly John and Mandy Southcott, Neil and Donna Forcer, Ian Hannent, Peter Ireland and everybody else. Special mention goes to Pat Price, now sadly no longer with us.

Thanks also to the efforts of Henry Wilson, Rupert Harding and Jane Robson of Pen and Sword who all helped make the writing of this book a joy.

Finally my family for support, proof reading, pictures, scanning: Mum, Dad, Tom, Rob and Jamie and finally Sheena, my wife, to whom this book is dedicated as a token of hers.

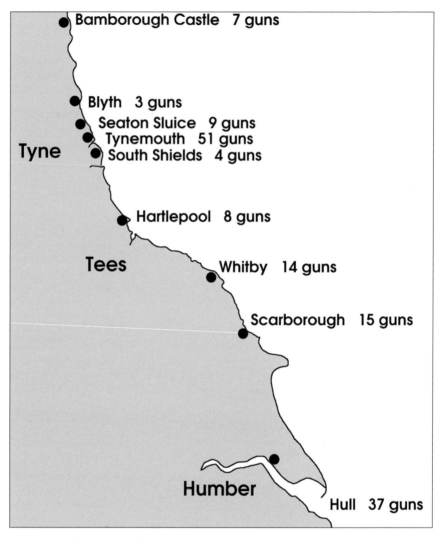

Napoleonic batteries on the North-East coast

HISTORY

So the history of Coast Artillery must largely be one of lonely garrisons vegetating for years in distant ports and batteries, of changes in organisation, methods, armament and fortification, and very rarely of the roar and smoke of battle and sudden death. (Colonel Maurice Jones, RA official historian)

VICTORIAN MUZZLE LOADING BATTERIES

During the Napoleonic Wars the coast of England was peppered with gun batteries to protect the shores from French incursion and around 170 guns were emplaced in the North-East alone. Following defeat of the French fleet at Trafalgar and the dispersal of her invasion force, 'The Army of England', in 1805, the threat evaporated. Final victory at Waterloo in 1815 led to the standing down of the region's defences and by 1817 the remaining guns had been withdrawn to depots at Berwick, Tynemouth and Scarborough. The batteries were closed, the Militia and Volunteers disbanded and a long peace followed.

Thirty-five years later, fears of French aggression stirred again. Sir Charles Napier, a much respected statesman, soldier and former military commander for the North of England, called for new preparations in a 'Letter on the Defence of England by Volunteer Corps and Militia'. Impressed by his arguments, the Duke of Wellington urged Parliament to consider the state of the defences and wrote to Sir John Burgoyne, the Inspector General of Fortifications, in 1846 to advocate a new force of 150,000 men. Initially Parliament proved reluctant but in 1852 finally passed an Act to raise the militia and place them under the control of the Secretary for War. Along with the infantry and yeomanry were twenty-nine corps of artillery from which men could be drawn to man any local defences. In the North-East they were the Durham Artillery Militia Corps raised at Bishop Auckland in July 1853, the Northumberland Corps formed at Tynemouth in July 1854 and the East and North Yorkshire Corps in 1860. The corps were made up of civilians and ex-soldiers who were paid to train for three to four weeks a year, commanded by officers from the local gentry and assisted by a regular adjutant and gunnery instructor from the Royal Artillery.

Burgoyne meanwhile sent out a committee to examine the existing fortifications and determine the work required to bring the nation's ports into a proper state of defence. He faced several problems. Artillery was developing rapidly and the new works had to be designed using whatever theories lay to hand, as little if any practical experience existed. He even went so far as to send subordinates to report on American defences, which were at that time considered the most advanced. It was also difficult to predict how the ports were going to develop over the next few years. In particular, the spread of the railway and the emerging iron and steel industries were causing massive expansion at several North-East ports. His report was presented to the Home Secretary, Lord Palmerston, at the end of 1854 but not reviewed until 1856.

The mid-nineteenth century was a period of European instability and friction between Austria and a fledgling Italy threatened war. With the old enemy France supporting the Austrians the public became concerned. Intellectual sympathy for Italy and contempt for France was agitated by Felice Orsini. Earlier he had made bombs in England and conceived an unsuccessful plot to assassinate Napoleon III. He was captured and his actions led to French calls for revenge on 'Perfidious Albion'. Having escaped from an Austrian prison he returned to tour Britain, giving lectures on 'Austrian despotism'. He visited the North-East in 1856 where he played to packed houses.

The Crimean War provided a short interlude as France and England formed an uneasy alliance to defeat Russia. France then began strengthening her Cherbourg naval base, which, coupled with deteriorating relations with Napoleon III, viewed by some in England as 'a mean and scheming adventurer', stoked fears of conflict. The crisis deepened when France launched the world's first semi-steam-powered ironclad, *La Gloire* in 1858. With such vessels, it was feared that the French could easily break a blockade of their ports, the preferred British tactic to deny control of the seas to an enemy. Lord Palmerston, now Prime Minister, riding the mood of the country, argued that as France was uncontainable and could attack at will, regardless of the weather, invasion was almost inevitable.

Great efforts were made to modernize the Navy, culminating in HMS *Warrior* launched in 1861, at the time the most powerful battleship afloat. She was well armed and carried substantial armoured protection. Her sea keeping was less good and her range limited but she laid down the pattern of freely moving heavily armoured ships with which any new defences would have to contend. *Warrior* actually took on a coast defence role. Described as 'a black snake among the rabbits' by Napoleon III, her sole purpose was to reduce the threat of invasion by patrolling the Channel.

In spite of Admiralty opinion that coast defence should be the sole responsibility of the Navy, Palmerston pushed ahead and set up a Royal Commission in 1859 to plan new fortifications for naval dockyards. The resulting Royal Commission Forts, Palmerston Forts, or even 'Palmerston's Follies', depending on point of view, were the largest public project undertaken to that date. Begun in 1860 they were more than an anti-invasion defence. The Navy was badly stretched by their home defence role and it was hoped that strong land-based defences would free ships to continue working overseas, consolidating the empire.

Construction on the North-East coast and at other smaller ports was not affected by the Royal Commission and began some time before the findings were released. The Palmerston Forts were massive in scale but Burgoyne's works were modest and often contained only a handful of guns. As such they were not intended to repel invasion but to assist the Royal and Merchant Navies by providing fortified harbours for use as places of refuge in times of emergency. As the whole coastline did not require defence, the less developed ports did not receive guns even if they had been equipped with batteries in the past.

Only four North-East ports were sufficiently developed to be of use to the Navy and require protection, the Tyne, Sunderland, Hartlepool and the Humber. Tynemouth Castle was to be rearmed, Sunderland and Hartlepool defended by two batteries each and a large fort would overlook the Humber. A small battery was mooted for the Tees at Cargo Fleet but the idea was not taken further due to the treacherous nature of the river. The rapid growth of all these ports meant that Burgoyne's recommendations would be substantially redrafted before any work was actually undertaken. A handful of old Napoleonic guns were still held in storage at Tynemouth and Scarborough Castles under the care of the Royal Artillery Invalids but such antiques had no place in the defences now being contemplated.

At the time that the batteries were being considered, great efforts were under way to develop a gun to replace the old smoothbore muzzle loaders which had now reached the limit of their design. Nevertheless, as the Navy had a huge surplus of smoothbores, it was these that were to be employed in the North-East.

Following the redrafting of Burgoyne's proposals, work to build the new batteries began in earnest in late 1859. In most cases land was donated or leased for nominal rents from the town corporations, often at sites which had held Napoleonic or even earlier works. The batteries were designed by the Royal Engineers and built by contracted labour, often Irish navvies, under their supervision. The relationship between the engineers and artillery, at that time the two most scientific branches of the army, was close. Modifications could not be made without the engineers' approval and at least one battery in any area was equipped with offices, stores and a workshop for them. Mounting the guns, known officially as 'repository' or to the gunners 'scotch up', was carried out by whoever was available, under the watchful eyes of the Coast Brigade.

Defences for the Humber were concentrated on the north bank of the river at Fort Paull, which mounted nineteen guns to protect the approaches to Hull. Hartlepool received three batteries, at the Lighthouse, Heugh and Fairy Cove, which mounted a total of nine guns. Sunderland was protected by four guns while Tynemouth Castle, which had held artillery since the sixteenth century, was reconstructed for approximately twenty guns along with barracks, magazines and workshops. All were armed with 68pr smoothbore muzzle loaders.

One question remained unresolved: who was to man the new forts? The Royal Commission had found that a major advantage of fortification was 'To enable a small body of troops to resist a superior force or to enable partly trained bodies of men to contend successfully with those more perfectly disciplined than themselves.' It concluded:

> There seems to be no reason to doubt that such forces as maybe got together from the Disembodied or less perfectly trained portion of the Militia would, with an admixture of regular soldiers, be able to defend our dockyards against superior numbers when fortified with due regard to these principles. (Ian Hogg, *Coast Defences of England and Wales 1856-1956* (David & Charles, 1974))

The Royal Artillery Invalids were reformed as the Coast Brigade in 1858 with the intention of maintaining the otherwise empty batteries. They were experienced

A 68pr gun manned by Volunteers at Heugh Battery during the 1870s.

artillerymen, retired from active service, and a handful were allocated to each district. Unlike the Militia they were paid a wage and accommodation was provided, either in nearby barracks or in a 'Master Gunners Residence', a small house at one of the batteries. They were never intended to provide the main force to man the works in time of war. These would come from the reconstituted Militia. Nevertheless the public had grave reservations about the Militia. Many considered them little more than the gentry's private army who in the past had been used to put down civil disorder with deadly effect and who could still be called out 'In all cases of rebellion or insurrection'. Such fear was not without foundation. In 1860 the Northumberland Artillery Militia were called out to assist at a riot at Tynemouth and South Shields where they 'maltreated' the local police, prompting angry calls for their removal or disbandment. They had also gained a not unjust reputation for drunken and rowdy behaviour and fighting in the streets was not uncommon. Of greater significance, their training was generally poor and many officers simply purchased their commissions without military experience or any knowledge of artillery, which was fast becoming a highly technical subject. The middle classes responded by forming rifle clubs and demanded the formation of a properly trained Volunteer Corps, preferably with officers chosen for competence. Their calls were finally heeded by the Government and on 12 May 1859 the Secretary for War wrote to the lord lieutenants of each county authorizing them to raise such a force, although no regulations governing them were laid down until 1863. The Volunteers could also be called out in times of rebellion but only if an invasion were imminent or under way.

The Artillery Volunteers were not assigned to coast defence but were formed as 'position' (mobile) batteries and given whatever weapons could be spared. Thus each corps acquired a motley collection of field and small ex-naval guns kept at drill halls and practice batteries which they set up at their own expense. Although technically officers did not buy their commissions, there was a sliding scale of financial worth which determined the rank a man could hold. Nor were any regular artillerymen assigned to the Volunteers and their services had to be bought in. During the 1870s, after the formation of the National Artillery Association, the Volunteers became very keen on competition shooting and soon became proficient on a wide range of coast defence guns. Eventually they began training at their local batteries and became nominally accepted as part of the local defence scheme. Nonetheless, the relationship between the Militia, Volunteers and the Royal Artillery remained ill defined throughout the nineteenth century in spite of numerous of attempts to reorganize them into a cohesive force.

The first round of reforms began in 1877 under Lord Cardwell, the Secretary of State for War. A keen supporter of land-based defence, his statement of 1871 brings to mind Churchill's famous speech of 1940:

> I believe if we agree to arm our population, as we propose to arm them, and if we avail ourselves of our national means of defence by placing torpedoes in all our harbours and rivers, and rifles behind our ditches and hedges the time has arrived when we no longer need to give way to

panic or fear of invasion.

Cardwell's reforms were well thought out and far reachcsing but, as they were instituted to save money, the potential to improve operational efficiency was not realized. He introduced short terms of service for regular personnel and linked overseas battalions with those at home to ease reinforcement. In terms of coast defence he set up a higher command with the establishment of artillery districts which incorporated the Militia and Volunteers. For the first time each district's corps became the responsibility of a single full-time senior officer, in most cases a lieutenant colonel in the Royal Artillery.

By the time of Cardwell's reforms the *Warrior* was long obsolete and a new class of ironclad had emerged against which the smoothbore gun was useless. One of Britain's latest vessels was HMS *Thunderer*, armed with powerful 12-in rifled muzzle loading (RML) guns. A pair in each turret weighed over 400 tons and the ship was protected by an armour belt up to 12 inches thick. A similar turret tested on the ranges at Shoeburyness had survived being fired on by 12-in shells at a range of only 200 yards, proving beyond any doubt that smoothbore coast defence guns were now insufficient.

The Navy had adopted the RML early but it was not until the 1870s that enough became available for the army to start replacing coast guns in the North-East. Mounting them in the existing batteries proved trivial, requiring only minor modifications and their introduction did not significantly alter the layout of the region's defence. The majority of RML guns mounted here were 64pr, converted from the 32pr smoothbore, with a sprinkling of 80pr RML converted from the 68pr smoothbore. As the new guns were rifled the Militia and Volunteers had no use for the old smoothbores which were scrapped or, as it was quaintly termed, 'brought to produce'. Unfortunately, many records from this time appear to be lost and the dates for the changeover in the region are not known.

In 1879 catastrophe struck HMS *Thunderer*. A gun was accidentally double loaded and exploded when fired, killing eleven men and wounding thirty. The double loading was caused by the hydraulic rams used to press cartridge and shell down the barrel and could not have happened with a breech loader. The Navy had already reached an impasse with the RML as its short barrel was not suited to firing new, more powerful, slow-burning powders. Krupp in Germany was successfully making BL guns with long composite steel barrels capable of firing the new powders and concerted efforts began to build a British 12-in primary gun for the Navy, along with a range of smaller guns for use as secondary armament. The hydraulic loading rams which had caused the explosion on *Thunderer* were not used in coast defence and indeed many of the problems encountered using RML guns in the confines of a ship did not apply on land. The Navy were quick to adopt the new breech loaders, creating a huge surplus of RML guns which soon found their way into land service.

An important turning point for coast defence came in 1882. Up to this time naval tactics had remained entrenched in the days of the 'wooden wall', with ships fighting in line and firing broadsides. This worked well, if only because brute force compensated for the inherent inaccuracy of the guns. In 1882 the Royal Navy bombarded Egyptian coast batteries at Alexandria with over 3,000 shells. Although the damage looked impressive and the garrison soon retreated, they had found the dispersed Egyptian guns extremely difficult to silence and many survived intact. Forward-thinking minds led by the newly appointed Inspector General of Fortifications, Sir Andrew Clarke, began considering a move away from massive works, as epitomized by the Palmerston Forts, towards smaller concealed defences.

During 1870s Captain Colin Scott Moncrief of the Edinburgh Artillery Militia had laid down some basic principles in his design for disappearing batteries, where a magazine was placed between a pair of guns and the overall height kept to a minimum. Such dispersed batteries were cheap, could be built almost anywhere and proved extremely hard to hit and almost impossible to destroy. From the artilleryman's point of view such a pair of guns, conveniently supplied by a central magazine was easily controlled by a single battery commander. Never fully accepted for the RML, the design was to prove ideal for the new breech loaders.

Even before Alexandria it had been realized that the existing fortifications were not sufficient and Lord Morley was selected to head a commission to examine the state of the nation's defences. The North-East was visited on his behalf by a subcommittee of Admiralty and Royal Engineer officers, comprising Vice Admiral Phillimore, Vice Admiral Boys and Colonel Nugent. Their brief was wide-ranging and they were given a free hand to recommend new building or the closure of existing works as they saw fit. The mix of weapons and types of fortifications they suggested highlights the difficulty they faced in coming to terms with the emerging technologies.

They visited Hull on 8 February 1883 and were welcomed by the Trinity Board, who provided the steam yacht, *Duke of Edinburgh* for their tour of inspection. Accompanied by Colonel Cox, commander of the Northern District Royal Engineers, and Captain Cator, the Conservator of the Humber, they steamed out from Hull in foul weather. Paull Point Battery was, they said, 'a most excellent position in advance of Hull for the defence of the upper waters leading to the town', while Stallingborough Battery was well placed if a little low-lying. They then headed towards Spurn Head and, although their examination was cut short by rough seas, they agreed that it was a suitable place for the mounting of guns:

But no work at Spurn Head would command the channel entrance, . . . If a work be placed upon the Spurn Head it should mount five of the longest ranging guns and two medium guns, and should be supported by a floating battery with gun and torpedo boats; but even then in the thick, but otherwise favourable, weather, a determined assailant might find his way in and get up, notwithstanding the removal of the buoys and leading marks and the extinction of the lights, for though the ordinary channel is near the Head, the water is open and bold until opposite Cleeness Sand; moreover there are a great number of fishing-smack masters who are able to bring in the largest vessels in any weather and at any time of tide and might not be proof against temptation.

They visited Grimsby the following day but found that the lack of decent bedrock precluded any building there on the grounds of cost. This suggests they were still considering traditional designs rather than Moncrief batteries which could be placed almost anywhere.

Arriving at Hartlepool on 11 February, they reviewed the existing batteries, stating that both the Heugh and now abandoned Fairy Cove Batteries should be upgraded to RML guns. They were slightly more vague regarding the Lighthouse Battery, saying 'it may perhaps be reconstructed for one heavy gun in shielded casemate'. Some consideration was given to replacing both the Heugh and Lighthouse Batteries with a work on the newly constructed breakwater, but this again was considered too expensive and mentioned only in passing in the report. The description of 'East Hartlepool', is noteworthy in light of the bombardment in 1914: 'The defect of these batteries is that they draw fire on East Hartlepool; this, however is unavoidable. East Hartlepool, moreover, is the least valuable portion of the port.' They were struck by the potential of the rapidly growing town and went on to make a rather startling proposal for a sea fort on Long Scar rocks.

The Sub-Committee examined the ground to the southward of West Hartlepool as far as Seaton Carew:

> Upon an eminence near, and in front of, the Seaton Lighthouse is a convenient position for a battery, and here might be placed two heavy MLR guns of 18 guns [sic] to fire upon the offing, and cross with the gun in the Lighthouse Battery at East Hartlepool, and two medium MLR guns to sweep the shore and keep off boats. This disposition of batteries would afford fair protection to the Port, and at moderate cost; but the Long Scar appears to offer so excellent a position for a work that the Sub-Committee are disposed to recommend it instead; it is 1,200 yards in advance of the battery at Seaton Carew, and it therefore keeps a hostile vessel so much further off, while in addition it has some bearing of the waters of the Tees Bay. A battery here should mount 3 heavy M.L.R. guns and 2 medium guns; it would cost £35,000 more than the battery at Seaton. (Sub-Committee for Defence of Commercial Ports, Morley Report (Feb. 1881: author's collection)

Morley agreed with many of the conclusions but in drafting his report substituted a number of breech-loading guns for RML. It was presented to the Spencer Cavendish, the Secretary of State for War, in 1884 and passed on to Sir Andrew Clarke for his comments. The Inspector General disagreed with a number of the proposals, particularly the sea forts, on the grounds of cost, and recommended that even more breech loaders be used. He also recognized the value of submarine mines and recommended their use for the first time.

Sir Andrew Clarke also revised the proposals for the Tyne, replacing the proposed 10.4-in BL guns with the newer 9.2-in BL gun. Nevertheless, as with the other North-East ports, neither Morley's nor the Inspector General's proposals were carried out, even though the Tyne was the home of Armstrong's ordnance works at Elswick and was:

> commercially of the highest importance . . . the principal outlet in the
> north of the iron and coal trade, manufactories and shipbuilding yards
> line its banks, higher up the river beyond the bridge is a private arsenal
> of the first order in which guns and materials of the heaviest and the
> most approved pattern are manufactured . . . The Tyne is easily defended,
> good and commanding positions are found on both sides of its mouth
> and its high banks cover the shipping in its waters.

Tynemouth Castle, Spanish Battery and Cliffords Fort were all armed with
smoothbores and it had been suggested that these be upgraded to RML guns of 10-
in and even 11-in calibre but the proposals had been ignored. Although the
batteries did receive RML guns as normal replacements for the smoothbores, these
were not the large calibre guns recommended, a fact which led to a lively exchange
of letters in the local papers.

In the North-East Morley's report was simply the start of a long process of
consideration and, following its review by the Secretary of State for War, the
Defence Committee and Inspector General, it was put to one side until 1888 when
a new committee was formed by the Royal Engineers and Royal Artillery.

Lord Morley had also been tasked with reviewing the organization of the forces
manning the defences, resulting in the garrison artillery being organized into
eleven brigades, with the North-East coming under the control of the 1st Northern
Brigade headquartered at Newcastle. The brigades were still subdivided into
artillery districts under a lieutenant colonel but now he was provided with a full-
time adjutant and small clerical staff. The Militia were at last officially incorporated
into the Royal Artillery as the junior brigades which in this area were:

2nd Brigade Northern Division Royal Artillery (M) (Durham)
3rd Brigade Northern Division RA (M) (Northumberland)
4th Brigade Northern Division RA (M) (Yorkshire)

This was a difficult time to redefine coast defence requirements. The old
infrastructure had easily been converted for RML guns but, as the ports had grown,
deficiencies in the batteries' locations were becoming apparent and new sites were
not easy to acquire as the best land was already in use. Also it was uncertain how
effective the RML would be in deterring a raid, while the new breech loader was
unproven in the coast defence role. During the three years of Morley's
investigation the breech loader went from being virtually unconsidered to being
the prime choice.

At the same time a new threat had arisen with the introduction of small fast
torpedo-carrying boats which could run the gauntlet of slow-firing guns to enter
the undefended inner waters of a port. Such an attack was also likely to occur
during the hours of darkness but effective solutions were now at hand. New
batteries containing short range, small calibre quick fire (QF) breech loading guns,
supplemented with minefields illuminated by searchlight, could be used to create
a well-defended channel.

BREECH LOADING BATTERIES

In 1887 the first useful breech loaders for coast defence were introduced, the 6pr Hotchkiss, a small quick fire gun, useful against torpedo boats and the larger 4.7-in gun. The ubiquitous 6-in gun had been in development since the early 1880s and the Mk VI was introduced to naval service in 1885 but it was not until 1889 that suitable land mountings became available. The choice for the North-East was the hydro pneumatic (HP) mount, a 'disappearing' design where the gun barrel appeared over the parapet only at the time of firing. The introduction of these guns required further consideration by the planners as, since they had a much higher rate of fire than the old muzzle loaders, fewer were required to defend a given area. Accuracy was enhanced with the introduction of the rangefinder in 1887 which, coupled with electric signalling, made control of the guns rapid and effective. Electricity also made searchlights feasible and detachments of Royal Engineers were set up to man them. These requirements for fewer guns, greater ammunition capacity, rangefinder posts, searchlights and electric power meant that upgrading the old batteries was not enough. A complete rebuild was required.

Experiments with submarine mines had been carried out as far back as 1863 but it was not until the early 1880s, with the harnessing of electricity for remote detonation, that they became viable. They were placed on the sea bed so that they could be exploded under an enemy vessel, the desired mine being selected by using a rangefinder. A safe channel was provided for friendly shipping but the intention was that, even were this known to an enemy, the light guns would drive them into the minefield. Submarine mining companies were initially formed within the Royal Engineers, but given the specialist nature of the task, which included sailing a mine-laying steamer, independent Militia and Volunteer units were soon formed. The Humber and Tees Divisions were created in 1886, followed

A typical early QF gun. This is a hotchkiss 3pr as used for practice in the North-East. Note the pistol grip and shoulder butt.

A typical mine-laying steamer, with two mines slung over the side, in 1889.

by the Tyne Division in 1888. To begin with they had no facilities but depots and guns were eventually set up. Fort Paull Submarine Mine Depot on the Humber was completed in 1886, South Gare on the Tees in 1892 and Cliffords Fort on the Tyne in 1893. Each was equipped with searchlights and a couple of small quick fire guns under Royal Artillery control along with a boat shed for the mine-laying steamer, accommodation and various stores.

The lack of any modern breech loading batteries in the region demanded that the defences be upgraded with some urgency. A Royal Artillery and Royal Engineers Works Committee was set up which studied the earlier proposals and promptly dismissed most of them. They rationalized the types of guns to be deployed, which were to be 9.2-in, 6-in or 6pr, with only a handful of RML to be left where a site was considered of little value to anyone but the Volunteers. For a change the majority of the proposals were accepted and the report paved the way for a complete reworking of the defences in the North-East. Commencing in 1890 work reached a peak in 1893 with the construction of new 6-in hydro pneumatic batteries on the Tyne and at Hartlepool, together with the reworking of Fort Paull on the Humber. The only real deviation from the plans was the use of a number of cheaper 4.7-in guns instead of the 6-in.

Edward Stanhope became Secretary of State for War in 1887. He was once considered one of Britain's finest war ministers but is now almost forgotten. Although a keen supporter of the Volunteers, he was unable to make good all their equipment or write off their debts, but he was able to secure a generous mobilization grant and provide some equipment, not least of which were 226 field guns. Other material was also released so that, for example, the Hull Artillery Volunteers received a pair of 64pr RML on proper traversing slides, allowing them to practise on the same equipment they would be expected to man if embodied. The following year saw an invasion scare, exacerbated by Lord Wolseley's maiden speech in the House of Lords, and the Volunteers' efficiency was evaluated with a series of 'surprise mobilization tests' when they were ordered to man their local defences overnight. The exercises appear to have been a success and may well have helped secure their role as part of the official defence when further reorganization was undertaken in 1889. Certainly this was the time when the Volunteers were properly integrated into home defence policy. The country was split into three divisions, each commanded by a colonel, Eastern with its HQ at Dover, Southern at Portsmouth and Western headquartered at Plymouth, but there was a depot at Scarborough to cover the North-East. Scarborough, although not equipped with fixed defences, had been the headquarters of the Yorkshire Militia since their inception. The units in the North-East now became:

Northumberland Artillery Western Division RA
Durham Artillery Western Division RA
Yorkshire Artillery Western Division RA

For the first time the regulars, Coast Brigade, Militia and Volunteers came under the command of the same officer, the Divisional CRA (Commander Royal Artillery). In 1891 further reorganization refined the divisional system and for the first time recognized specialists, such as telephonists, range finders and machine gunners, with higher rates of pay. One side effect of the reorganization was that the Volunteers of the Humber Division submarine miners were found to be inefficient and replaced by the Militia. The artillery Volunteers, however, had proven themselves very competent and in recognition of this were renamed the Volunteer Artillery.

It was Stanhope's work in reshaping the War Office, the supply of armaments and his distrust of the existing Defence and Mobilization Committees that paved the way for coast defence to enter the breech loading age and thus the twentieth century. For the first time the army and Navy would cooperate fully and a Joint Naval and Military Commission was set up to consider the coast defences, a precurser to the Committee of Imperial Defence.

No matter what improvements were made in coast defence, the navies were always one step ahead and ironclads were generally sufficiently armed to outgun and outrange most batteries. Upgrading the defences was a primary concern but agreement was rare as technology continually moved forward and no one could really anticipate future requirements. In most cases no attempt was made to match the ironclads' firepower and there are a number of good reasons for this. Given that a battery was so hard to destroy, an enemy vessel should be engaged for as long as it remained in range and to suffer such fire, even from a small calibre gun, could be expected to act as a deterrent, particularly as she then had to limp home. Common sense would dictate that the aggressor only had to stay out of range but, given the difficulty of aiming from a moving ship, identifying suitable targets and observing fall of shot, the effectiveness of any such long-distance bombardment would be a gamble at best. Also, although the reports often indicate the commercial value of a port, coast defence was still solely concerned with providing protection to the Navy by providing refuge. Defence against long-range saturation bombardment remained the perogative of the Navy.

In 1894 the Royal Artillery and Royal Engineers Works Committee was reformed to review their work of 1888 which had established the breech loading batteries and finally get rid of any remaining RML guns. Their report entitled *Substitution of BL and QF Guns for Heavy and Medium RML Guns on Sea Fronts* provides us with a comprehensive snapshot of the state of the region's defences:

Humber:

Paul's Point Battery, two 4.7-in guns with three 6-in to be added
Volunteer Practice Battery, four 64pr RML

Tees:

South Gare Battery, two 4.7-in, two 6pr
Lighthouse Battery, one 6-in (Awaiting mounting)
Heugh Battery, three 64pr RML to be replaced with two 6-in
Cemetery Battery, two 6-in BL
Seaham
North and South Batteries, four 64pr RML (Volunteer training)
Sunderland
Wave Basin Battery, four 80pr RML, one 3pr QF
Abb's Point Battery, three 64pr RML to be closed

Tyne:

Cliffords Fort, two 6pr QF
Frenchman's Point, under construction, one 8-in and two 6-in proposed

Three 6-in guns not mentioned in the report were at the time being mounted at Tynemouth Castle and Spanish battery. Although the report was concerned with removing the RML guns, the rationalization was incomplete as, excluding the Volunteers' 64pr guns, the North-East would still have six different types of gun, including the 8-in BL and 80pr RML. Servicing such a wide range of guns was becoming a major task for the Coast Brigade who had to deal with multiple calibre shells and all the spares and equipment required to keep each in service. The final report of the century was undertaken by Montgomery in 1899 and his summary of each port's significance is included in the Gazetteer.

The establishment of the hydro pneumatic batteries created the pattern of defence which would continue until the First World War but the guns themselves were very soon outdated and the turn of the century saw yet another round of upgrades. The original 6-in guns were black powder weapons introduced just as cordite was coming into service and, although they could fire reduced charges, the result was reduced barrel life. The hydro pneumatic mount also reduced the rate

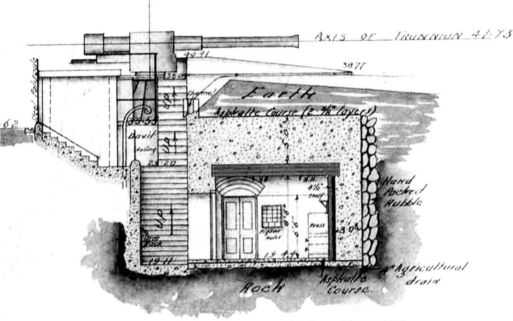

A 6-in Mk VII with magazine underneath at Lighthouse Battery 1900.

of fire and in later reports such guns are invariably referred to as being on slow mountings. In 1898, a new 6-in gun was introduced by Vickers which could be mounted on a simple central pivot mount. Known as the 6-in Mk VII this weapon became the workhorse of the garrison artillery and served through two world wars until closure of the batteries in 1956. Work to install at the old RML and at new sites began in 1900 and was largely completed by 1902 to be followed by replacement of the obsolete HP guns between 1905 and 1907. The last of the RML guns removed in these years were issued to the Volunteers for practice and continued in service or languished in drill halls for a surprising number of years. Indeed, it was not until 1921 that the army finally struck the last of them from the books.

In the early years the function of the batteries was relatively simple, to prevent hostile vessels from closing on a port to inflict damage. The age-old problem was how to effectively identify an enemy before they attacked and equally worrying was the threat of equipment or spies being landed in peacetime. The answer lay in closer cooperation with the coastguard, who were already charged with controlling shipping entering or leaving ports. Coastguard stations were equipped with semaphore and signalling lamps with which to challenge shipping and also an examination vessel to approach and if necessary board any suspect ship. The setting up of the examination service extended the arm of the coastguard by giving them access to a battery gun with which to fire warning shots and, if necessary, sink a vessel not complying with their instructions. Ideally, two batteries were required, the examination battery with the gun to fire the warning shots and the selected battery to provide heavy fire as a back up. An immediate problem was identifying which battery should be used to provide the examination gun. Quick fire was desirable and small calibre, as less damage was done if the vessel turned out to be friendly. In fact, over the years the batteries damaged far more friendly than enemy ships! Often the chosen gun did not fit these requirements and a smaller field gun was employed instead. Also, it was desirable that the examination battery was fitted with searchlights, with their associated detachment of Royal Engineers, but this was not always the case.

An effective examination service depended on the telephone for real time communication between the various coastguard signal stations and the Admiralty and they were the first organization to have such a network. The lines spread out later to include the batteries, although semaphore continued in use for many years at some batteries. The coastguard themselves controlled shipping in their vicinity by semaphore and a system of coloured lights: so, for example, if they wished to close the harbour three vertical red lights would be displayed. Port war signal stations for the coastguard were initially set up in any suitable building, with lighthouses being pressed into service at the start of the First World War until purpose-built towers were erected. The examination service was a continual service although it should be remembered that the batteries were only involved when the gunners were mobilized, in other words, in time of war.

At the turn of the century it was decided that the British Army was yet again in need of modernization. Coast artillery had proved unpopular with many officers who preferred the dashing image of the horsed artillery. Although the Volunteers and Militia remained keen, the situation was so bad that regular officers now found themselves posted to the garrison artillery as a form of punishment. Major

Volunteers practising on a 16pr RML. Several such guns were used temporarily as the examination gun where the emplaced gun was unsuitable.

General Arbuthnot, appointed to consider the problem in 1882, had summed the situation up thus:

> The garrison artillery, the most scientific branch of the arm and which should command the services of the best officers, instead of being sought after, is shunned, and if priority of choice were given to young officers on joining the Regiment according to their places in the batch, the best would select the field artillery, and the garrison artillery, which requires the most scientific officers, would only get those who, from idleness or want of ability, had failed to obtain a good place in their batch. (M. Jones, *History of Coast Artillery in the British Army* (Royal Artillery Institution, 1959)

It was decided to create separate corps and in June 1899 the Regiment of Artillery was split into the Royal Horse and Royal Field Artillery and the Royal Garrison Artillery. As an incentive garrison artillery officers received a pay rise and a nurturing of pride in the new corps significantly improved morale. The result in the North-East was reorganization of the gunners, resulting in the formation of the Northumberland Royal Garrison Artillery, the Durham RGA and East Riding of Yorkshire RGA, incorporating the Militia and Volunteers and District Establishments

The old divisions were reorganized as groups and the North Eastern Group had its headquarters and depot at Scarborough. After forty-four years the value of the Volunteer Artillery was finally recognized in July 1903, when the War Office called for the formation of Volunteer Special Service Sections to serve in case of emergency. Their status was confirmed with further reorganization in 1905 when the Special Service Sections were abolished and the Volunteers officially incorporated into the new Coast Defence Commands, with all the region's forces coming under the control of Tyne Coast Defence Command.

Between 1902 and 1907 the regions defences were reviewed on an annual basis by Major General 'Fred' Slade, the Inspector of the Royal Garrison Artillery. He presented wide-ranging accounts and personal recommendations for his superiors. The RGA were, he said, stretched with too few resources and he urged 'most strongly that one of the surplus Royal Garrison Artillery companies now being withdrawn from stations abroad should be sent to Newcastle'.

At this time the whole region was only served by two district officers and their detachments, who although 'thoroughly efficient, and the works and batteries are in a very clean and satisfactory state' were not sufficient to secure this extended command.

In 1905 he began his tour with Colonel Kidd of the Tynemouth RGA Volunteers and saw a mock attack by HMS Dryad which steamed slowly into the harbour, 'firing' at the batteries as she went. Slade was very impressed by the Volunteers who he found to be both smart and capable and watched a very satisfactory practice on the 6-in guns.

He was unable to see the Tees defences in action as the batteries were unmanned, the Volunteers could not afford it and an examination vessel was not available. He had to content himself with visiting the empty batteries and reading

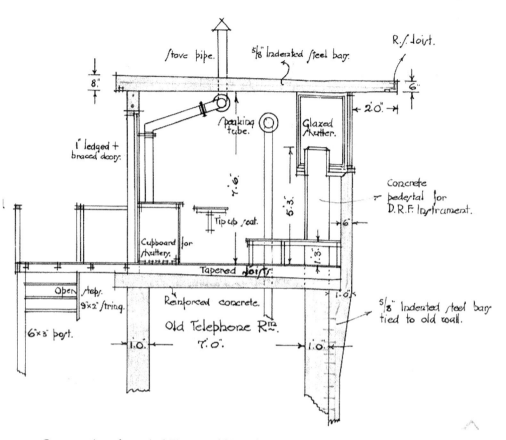

Cross-section of a typical First World War battery command post containing a depression rangefinder.

the fort record books. Although liberal with his praise for the garrison he was again concerned at the lack of resources and distances involved for essential repairs:

There is only one No. 5 Ordnance workshop at Hartlepool, and all repairs to armament, &c., which cannot be carried out in such a workshop have to be done at Tynemouth, 35 miles from Hartlepool and 56 miles from South Gare (including 5 miles by road). I suggest the existing No. 5 shop be altered to a No. 4 shop, which would permit of all ordinary repairs being carried out locally, and that a drilling machine should also be supplied. *(Report by Major General F G Slade, CB, Inspector of Royal Garrison Artillery, on his Inspection of the North-Eastern District, 25th to 27th July 1904. PRO WO 27/490)*

Paull Point Battery was being reconstructed when Slade visited and he was disappointed with what he found. The heavy gyn needed to lift the guns into place had been delayed, the ammunition stores were incomplete, and there was also no No. 4 Workshop so, once again, major repairs had to be carried out at Tynemouth, 140 miles away. There was also the perennial problem of essential equipment being held back. At Tynemouth he found that the electric firing gear for the 9.2-in guns had been on order for four years! The main problem, though, was the lack of an effective command structure:

> The general condition of the armament, ammunition, stores, and equipment in the North Eastern District is very satisfactory, considering that there are only two officers of the Royal Garrison Artillery employed in the care of the same, one in charge of Paull Point Battery and one in charge of all the other works, and both of these District Officers.

> The fact of the CRA and Staff Officer of the North Eastern District both belonging to the Royal Field Artillery, and there being no Instructor of Gunnery and Range Finding, entails greater responsibility on these district Officers, as they are really their advisors on Royal Garrison Artillery and coast defence questions. *(Report by Lieut-General F G Slade, CB, Inspector of Royal Garrison Artillery, on his Inspection of the Newcastle-on-Tyne Defences, 26th to 29th July 1905. PRO WO 27/494)*

As part of the ongoing reviews of Britain's armed forces, the Owen report of 1905 was particularly brief and to the point. All ports were downgraded to Class C status, many guns were to go and the phrase 'considered superfluous' appears throughout. In fact, the only new guns advocated in the region were two batteries of two 6-in Mk VII to protect Sunderland. The committee under General Sir John Owen had undertaken a hardnosed but realistic examination and decided to sweep the defences of obsolete or unnecessary weapons. Some sites were upgraded but if a location was questionable it was to be closed and not allowed to linger on. It was the same with the 6pr guns which were no longer powerful enough to combat the destroyer and all were removed. The Navy classified ports by their liability to certain forms of attack and Owen's decisions were based on the theoretical role of three guns.

> Class A attack. Bombardment at long range by battleships or heavy cruisers. 9.2-in required.
> Class B Attack. Bombardment at medium range by light cruisers. 6-in required.
> Class C Attack. Attempt to break down naval obstructions or block the entrance to a port or harbour. 4.7-in required.

They were well aware that the 4.7-in was not powerful enough and so did not recommend removal of the 6-in guns in the Class C ports. By not requiring 6-in guns for Class C ports they saved having to replace any existing 4.7-in guns.

The recommendations were not popular with the region's officers and this found voice in Major General Jason Dalton's report of 1906:

> I regret, that as a result of the recommendations of General Owen's Committee, a considerable reduction of armament in this command has been decided on. I only hope that the guns down for reduction may, in most cases, be retained as reserve guns and left available for the drill and instruction of the Volunteers. These northern Volunteer Corps are very efficient and keen; they take great pride in being allotted to the defence of their own part of the country, and I should be sorry to see them discouraged. The 2nd East Yorkshire RGA Volunteers are especially energetic and enterprising under the command of Colonel Lambert White; and have a model drill hall at Hull, replete with ingenious and costly contrivances put up at their own cost for instruction in coast defence. I understand that my predecessor, Lieut.-General Slade, drew attention to this. (*Report by Major-General J C Dalton, Inspector Royal Garrison Artillery, on his Inspection of the Newcastle-on-Tyne Defences, 26th to 29th September 1906.* PRO WO 27/493)

General Owen had optimized and, it must be said, improved the command, but with less guns fewer men were required, a dismaying prospect for the Volunteers whose future was already in the balance as complete reorganization of the army was considered.

PREPARING FOR WAR

Piecemeal reorganization of the armed forces had not been a success and following the Boer War it was realized that a complete overhaul was required, which included bringing the Volunteer and Militia corps into line with the regular services. In fact, when the Militia had been mobilized to man the coast defences during the Boer War they had been unprepared and shown themselves unable to carry out the role with any efficiency.

Committees were set up to review both operational status and equipment and in 1906 reforms were put in place by the Secretary of State for War, Richard Haldane, which split the army into two groups, the Expeditionary Force, or regular army for overseas service, and a new Territorial Force which came into being on 1 April 1908. Included in the Territorial Force were 'special troops for defended ports', comprising 'such artillery and engineers as could not be provided by divisions'. In fact, the old Volunteer Artillery signed up en masse in this region and reformed as the East Riding, Durham and Tynemouth RGA (TF). A second, short-lived force was also set up and the majority of the region's Militia Artillery transferred to the Special Reserve Royal Field Artillery before being summarily disbanded in 1909. The Submarine Miners had been abolished in 1907 and, having been transferred to the Electrical Engineers, were reformed as the Durham Fortress Engineers to man and maintain the searchlights.

The Territorials were designated for home defence but if 90 per cent of a unit volunteered they could then apply to be placed on the Imperial Service list and be liable to serve abroad during times of war. There is little evidence that the region's coast gunners volunteered, probably because they expected to man their local batteries during wartime.

Britain's industrial might in the latter half of the nineteenth century had created the world's most powerful navy and a French school of thought, the Jeune École led by Rear Admiral Theophile Aube, attempted to overturn this imbalance by adopting and creating tactics for new weapons which were beginning to appear. Unable to match Britain ship for ship they declared the battleship obsolete and that the mine, torpedo and submarine would dominate future naval tactics. Nor were these to be used solely against an opponent's navy: they would also attack and cripple the enemy's merchant fleet. The Jeune École believed that expediency overruled moral qualms and all means possible should to be used to conclude a war quickly. This included the bombardment of enemy ports, fortified or not, for material effect or even ransom.

Aube, the French Minister of Marine, began cancelling capital ship programmes in 1886 and ordered large numbers of fast cruisers and torpedo boats. He was, unfortunately, just too far ahead of his time. The technology was in its infancy, the new torpedo boats were barely seaworthy and suitable motors didn't even exist for the submarines. His tenure lasted only eighteen months and he was superseded by a far more traditionally minded officer. Nevertheless, as the technologies matured, the theories of the Jeune École grew in importance, and in identifying the vulnerability of a merchant fleet they had accurately named the greatest threat to Britain. First Sea Lord, John Arbuthnot 'Jackie' Fisher, clearly understood the threat and in 1904 stated:

The Navy is the 1st, 2nd, 3rd, 4th, 5th . . . ad infinitum line of defence!

If the Navy is not supreme, no army however large is of the slightest use. It is not invasion we have to fear, IT'S STARVATION. (A J Marder, *From Dreadnought to Scapa Flow*, vol. 1, *The Road to War* (Oxford University Press, 1961)

Defeat in the Franco-Prussian War and the chaos of the ensuing Paris Commune had seen the threat from France rapidly diminish and the focus of Britain's fears shifted to the newly created Germany. Led by Krupp, an arms race had germinated which, coupled with the German state's desire for empire, was ultimately to lead to the so-called Great War. To military planners at the end of the century conflict seemed almost inevitable. In 1898 Tirpitz, the German Minister of Defence, wrote:

For Germany the most dangerous naval enemy at the present time is England . . . Our fleet must be constructed so that it can unfold its greatest military potential between Heligoland and the Thames . . . The military situation against England demands battleships in a great a number as possible. *(Marder, From Dreadnought to Scapa Flow, vol. 1)*

In 1906 Britain finally brought the diverse technologies of the ironclad together into a cohesive whole with the launching of HMS *Dreadnought*, outdating all other battleships at a stroke. Germany rapidly copied the design but had one serious obstacle to overcome: the recently constructed Kiel Canal was too narrow for the new vessels. 'Jackie' Fisher saw the writing on the wall and predicted in 1906 that when work to widen the Kiel Canal was completed in October 1914, 'the Battle of Armageddon' would break out. In fact, the First World War began in August.

While the naval arms race gathered pace, little was done to improve land-based defences. It was understood that their static nature was a major drawback, not simply because the guns were immobile but also because change incurred significant expense. Suitable mobile guns, the largest of which was the 4.7-in, lacked the necessary range or power and it was decided to extend the reach of the protected ports by equipping them with light cruisers, destroyers and submarines under the Coastal Patrol Organization inaugurated in 1908.

The introduction of the coastal patrol underscored the increasing complexity of coast defence, leading to a reappraisal of its organization. Matters were complicated as the batteries had to work with the Navy, coastguard, and other army detachments, in particular, the engineers operating the searchlights and infantry protecting the flanks. The solution lay in enabling these services to work together effectively and, using telephones and semaphore, a sophisticated command and control system was developed. Each defended port was placed under a fortress command to act as a clearing house for intelligence and generate any orders required. The batteries were grouped in fortresses by the areas of sea they covered, each under a fire commander reporting directly to the fortress commander. In the smaller ports, which includes all those in this region, the director in charge of the searchlights reported in the first instance to fortress command and also to the local fire commander when required, while infantry reported to fortress command only. The port war signal station, operated by the coastguard, was independent,

This picture shows men practising on the dummy loader in 1934. Behind are: left, the battery command post and, right, fire commander's post and port war signal station.

reporting only to the Admiralty. However, as it coordinated the working of the examination service, direct links were established with the nearest fire commander.

The system matured in the years just before the war with the introduction of radio direction finding stations which listened for radio signals from hostile shipping and tracked their location by means of triangulation. Following the capture of German code books in August and October 1914, reports were telegraphed to Room 40 at the Admiralty in London, where they were decoded, filtered and interpreted to generate orders for the Navy and warnings for the army.

Theories regarding the Navy's role in the defence of Britain had long polarized into two factions. The traditionalists, now led by Fisher and known as the 'Blue Water' school maintained that the Navy was supreme. Opposing them, the 'Bolt from the Blue' school feared that, as the rules of war were not sufficiently resolved, an enemy might attempt to launch an invasion and strike a crippling blow before war had actually been declared. Given the time required to organize an invasion and the necessity of holding off the defender's fleet, the Blue Water theories were generally held to be correct but in 1912 it was decided to put them to the test and during the summer large-scale manoeuvres were carried out in the North Sea. These highlighted problems with the Blue Water theories, as part of the 'invasion' force was able to lie unmolested off Filey. The exercise was repeated the following year and this time the results were damning: 48,000 troops were able to 'land' at Sunderland and Blyth; an invasion force attacking the Humber was stopped by torpedoes but the fleets did not clash as expected. In fact, not only were the defending fleet unable to locate the 'enemy', they were severely mauled by 'hostile' submarines. The Blue Water school was roundly criticized by Callaghan, the Commander in Chief of Home Fleets:

> The only proper defence against Invasion and raid is by military forces, and to make the Navy responsible for this work is a grave strategic error, which hands the initiative wholly to the enemy. Given that the country is able to look after itself on shore, our fleet can ensure the complete destruction of German seaborne trade. (Marder, *From Dreadnought to Scapa Flow*, vol. 1)

Admiral of the Fleet, Sir William May, the Umpire in Chief, was more specific and he highlighted a key problem that had dogged the defenders, the inability to locate an enemy in fog:

> Provided that the attack is a surprise may be partially successful, especially in misty weather. The Coastal Patrol is not sufficient. It therefore appears necessary to have fixed defences at the principal sea ports in the United Kingdom and of sufficient strength to be able to check a determined raid for some hours until a battlefleet can be concentrated on the spot.

Regardless of the warning bells rung by the Admiralty, no plans were put in place to bring the defences up to the standard required for a major war.

THE FIRST WORLD WAR

At the outbreak of the First World War the defences for the North-East were:

Tyne Defended Port, manned by No 12 and 47 Company RGA (Regular) and
   Tynemouth RGA (Territorial).
Tynemouth Castle, one 9.2-in Mk X, two 6-in Mk VII
Frenchman's Point Battery, one 9.2-in Mk X, two 6-in Mk VII (actually manned
   by Durham RGA)
Spanish Battery, two 6-in Mk VII
Tees and Hartlepool Defended Port manned by Durham RGA (Territorial)
Heugh Battery, two 6-in Mk VII
Lighthouse Battery, one 6-in Mk VII
South Gare Battery, two 4.7-in
Humber Defended Port manned by East Riding RGA (Territorial)
Fort Paull, three 6-in Mk VII
Spurn Head, four 4.7-in

The start of war prompted attempts to bring the defences up to their recommended strength, but to begin with this comprised little more than siting a few light guns and searchlights on an ad-hoc basis under the direction of local commanders. Trenches were dug and field guns placed along the coast. These were not so much anti-invasion measures but used to provide work and training for men recruited as part of Kitchener's army. One glaring deficiency, noted just before the outbreak of war, was at the Humber where the Navy had established an oil fuel depot at Immingham. Only a handful of 6-in and 4.7-in guns were in place and work commenced on two batteries to replace Fort Paull which was too far upriver. Harking back to Morley's report of 1881, a proposal to build two sea forts to close the mouth of the river was backed by the First Sea Lord, Winston Churchill. Bull Sand and Haile Forts were to be the most expensive fortifications built in the North-East.

The First World War saw the first seaborne raids against Britain since the French landings at Fishguard in 1797. The Bombardment of Hartlepool on 16 December 1914 was the only classic dual ever fought between British mainland shore batteries and capital ships. The attack is covered in detail and brief mention is given of other raids later.

The bombardment of the North-East coast brought to light many deficiencies, as the attack was considerably heavier than expected and the fleet too far distant to arrive in time. The value of fixed defences had come under intense scrutiny during the early months of the war when French land fortresses had rapidly and unexpectedly fallen. Even so, the British naval attack on the Dardanelles in 1915, prelude to the disastrous landings at Gallipoli, had been repulsed with heavy losses by coast defences. This led the War Council to examine the effectiveness of naval guns against howitzers in attacking various types of fort. They concluded

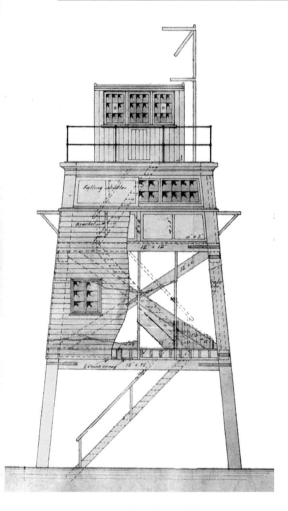

A combined First World War fire command post and port war signal station at Heugh Battery.

that in a land battle, where howitzers could be brought to bear, even the strongest forts were vulnerable, but ships' guns, 'owing to the small angle of descent are not able to attack concealed forts and batteries . . . but provided their gun power is greater than that of the forts, the ships could keep out of range' (Lord Kitchener and Winston Churchill, *The Dardanelles* (TSO Publishing, 2000); reprint of *The Dardanelles Commission*, part 1 (HMSO, 1917)).

It was concluded that the existing batteries were worth retaining but simply did not have the range to keep an aggressor at bay and the decision was taken in 1915 to create a number of 'counter bombardment' batteries. The largest of these in Britain were the Tyne Turrets, built north and south of the river, each mounting a complete 12-in gun turret taken from a redundant warship. Hartlepool and the Tees received 9.2-in guns on high angle mountings at the Palliser and Pasley Batteries, while the Humber was equipped with four 9.2-in guns, in Kilnsea and Green Batteries at either end of Spurn Head. Apart from the Humber sites, which were begun in 1915, work did not commence until 1918 and the guns were not operational until the early 1920s.

The First World War also brought the new threat of attack from the air and the garrison artillery found themselves responsible for manning anti-aircraft guns. Initially a number of guns were pressed into service which would have been familiar to the gunners, the most impressive being twelve 6-in guns transferred from the Navy and mounted on railway trucks in 1915. To fight the Zeppelins they also manned 12pr guns and a number of 3pr mounted on the back of lorries, while the Royal Engineers manned hastily erected searchlights.

A 6-in anti-aircraft gun, one of twelve transferred from the Navy to the army in 1915. The gun was at Port Clarence on the Tees. A similar gun at Saltburn was later sent to the Western Front. The gun was a quick firer and used a brass cartridge. Note the collar on the muzzle which took a rope so that the barrel could be depressed by men pulling. The conversions were carried out at Darlington.

Of course, manning the guns and undertaking the extra duties consumed a large number of fit professional gunners who were better deployed abroad. The batteries became nurseries for new recruits who were then dispatched to heavy and siege batteries on the Western Front. Many of the original gunners volunteered to serve overseas in 1915 and the batteries were then manned by a steady flow of men training to join the siege batteries under the watchful eyes of those too old or otherwise disbarred from overseas service. The Durham RGA alone trained over 2,000 men.

BETWEEN THE WARS

German defeat and the scuttling of her fleet at Scapa Flow in June 1919, along with chaos of Revolutionary Russia, at a stroke removed any naval threat to Britain in European waters. An attempt was made to prevent the outbreak of a new naval arms race with the Five Power Naval Treaty signed in 1922 between Britain, America, Japan, France and Italy. This limited the maximum size of new battleships to 35,000 tons and set the permissible ratio of vessels between the five states. It remained in force until 1934 when Japan reneged, simultaneously throwing open competition not only from the signatories but also Germany. For Britain, as the foremost naval power, serious post-First World War competition came only from America and Japan and were these two countries to go to war the conflict would inevitably take place in the Far East. In recognition of Britain's interest there, the focus of coast defence policy shifted to Singapore where it was decided to build a powerful fortress. Although work did not begin in earnest until 1932, its necessity prevented coast defence from falling into complete decline and the need for men trained on the big guns allowed many batteries to continue operating.

Some guns were withdrawn, mainly those that had been set up for the duration of the war, along with some of the counter-bombardment batteries. The Territorials remained popular, particularly where batteries had been long established and volunteering had become a tradition. Although coast defence did not fall into decline, financial constraints prevented physical growth and the main inter-war

9.2-in gun being fired by Durham Heavy Brigade in 1934.

developments were in control and organization.

At the end of war the batteries had been put on a maintenance footing and left unmanned until the resurrection of the Territorial Force as the Territorial Army in 1920. After some small changes, the RGA was substantially reorganized in 1924 to reflect the fact that 80 per cent of the force was now mobile and the Royal Artillery was reunited for the first time since the split of 1899. Coast defence became the responsibility of the Heavy Brigades (TA) who were designated as heavy batteries in line with the rest of the Royal Artillery. They were expected to serve both in their local gun batteries and also on heavy guns in the field if required. In 1926 it was decided that responsibility for coast defence should be completely handed over to the Territorials, except for command and the specialist occupations which would still be undertaken by regulars. When implemented in 1927 the organization structure for each of the three defended ports in the North-East became:

Headquarters and staff: under command of a major, to become Commander Coast Defences on mobilization
District establishment: one complete detachment of instrument specialists per rangefinder, a master gunner and his maintenance staff
Manning details: the Territorials with their COs acting as fire commanders

The 1930s saw economy measures begin to take effect. First, the Territorials were themselves reorganized and diminished in 1932 to reflect their peacetime role and cost cutting led to reductions in live firing and other exercises. The gunners received an annual allowance of ammunition from which all rounds, whether fired at home or at camp, had to be taken, often leaving them very short and making practice at their own batteries very difficult. The situation was formalized during the national financial crisis of 1931 when 'Drill Years' were introduced, with live firing only allowed in alternate years.

The emplacement of new guns or any major modification was rare and expenditure was dependent on the role of a battery, with training taking precedence over defence. The regiments attended a number of camps during the year, some at their own batteries but more importantly the annual summer camp held at one of the larger sites where two or more brigades could assemble. For the men of the North-East this was usually Tynemouth Castle but they also travelled further afield, particularly to North Foreland at Dover and Inchkieth on the Forth.

Loading 'Old Bess', the 9.2-in gun at Tynemouth.

These all held the Territorials' beloved 9.2-in gun, the familiar 6-in gun and a range of smaller calibre weapons and it was here that new fire schemes, rangefinding and plotting techniques were introduced to the gunners.

The concept of counter-bombardment was formalized in the early 1930s and two types of battery were proposed. To increase the range, 9.2-in guns were to be placed on 35 degree mountings and 6-in guns on 45 degree mountings. Old 9.2-in guns were to be removed or remounted while the 15 degree 6-in guns would be reclassified as 'Close Defence' batteries. The range of the counter-bombardment guns was at the extreme limits of the existing rangefinders and a new system of controlling the guns, the fortress plotting system, was developed. This relied on discrete fortress observation posts feeding data via plotting rooms which in turn controlled the guns. The system was introduced in 1934 and a number of practice plotting rooms were set up in local drill halls. In fact, the system remained largely theoretical as the new rangefinders remained unfitted until the late 1930s and proper plotting rooms were not erected until the outbreak of war. (Gun control and the fortress plotting system are discussed in Chapter 2.)

Also around this time the gunners began to receive their first training in anti-aircraft defence, although only on the Lewis gun which proved very popular and became an important part of regimental competitions. It was considered important enough that in 1936 each brigade was allotted an extra twelve men as Lewis gunners.

As war approached, the gunners found themselves with extra duties. A minimum of training was given in gas and passive air defence and with the formation of the ARP services it fell to the gunners to tour factories and schools and impart this knowledge to the local population.

War came early to the batteries with the Munich Crisis in September 1938 when fear that war was about to break out led to the mobilization of the Territorials. Although they stood down two weeks later, valuable lessons were learnt and officers appointed, preparing the batteries for the long watch that lay ahead.

A proposed fortress command post for the Lighthouse Battery with (1) a depression rangefinder and (2) a Barr and Stroud. Several plans for such prestigious buildings were drawn up but none built, due to financial restraints.

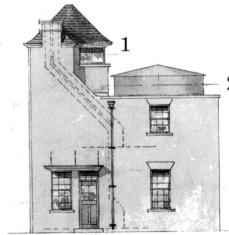

THE SECOND WORLD WAR

The situation that faced the coast gunners of 1939 was very different than that that had faced those of 1914. Coastal raiding was now unlikely as the German Navy was significantly weaker and air raid was the most efficient form of attack. Because of the risk posed by a coast artillery searchlight leading a night bomber to its target, they were removed from the fortress commanders' control and placed directly under HQ control. Written permission, or receipt of the correct codeword, was required for them to be lit. In the North-East 'Julius' was to be used if there were indications of an attack and 'Caesar' would be broadcast when invasion was imminent.

The implications of the fall of France in May 1940 seem to have taken both Britain and Germany by surprise. Britain had expected the war to follow the same pattern as the First World War, with a fixed Franco-Belgian front line, but now found its south coast wide open to invasion. Germany, expecting a rapid peace treaty, had barely considered the prospect. Following Dunkirk, Britain did not have the troops or equipment required for effective defence and the burden fell to the RAF to maintain air superiority to foil any attempt. Fortunately, but unknown to Britain, Operation Sealion, the German invasion plan, was little more than an amalgamation of unrelated ideas and projects drawn up by the German army, navy and air force, in the face of this unexpected opportunity.

Realizing the desperation of the situation, Churchill delegated General Ironside to execute a makeshift policy which attempted to bring the whole of the country into a state of defence. Hundreds of miles of fortifications were thrown up, with whatever materials were at hand, and with the formation of the LDV, later the Home Guard, the troops to man them were trained and armed. Much of this was done on an ad-hoc basis under difficult conditions, but it was no idle boast when Churchill claimed 'we will fight them on the beaches.' A minute entitled 'Defence against Invasion', written by Churchill in August 1940 to his Chiefs of Staff, shows just how important he considered the defence of the North-East:

> From Cromarty Firth to the Wash is the second most important sector, ranking next after the Wash to Dover. Here however all the harbours and inlets are defended, both from the sea and the rear, and it should be possible to counter attack in superior force within twenty-four hours. The Tyne must be regarded as the second major objective after London, for here (and to a lesser extent at the Tees) grievous damage could be done by an invader or large scale raider in a short time. (*The Second World War*, vol. 2, *Their Finest Hour* (Cassell & Co., 1949))

The British Expeditionary Force in France had already faced the problem of stopping the German advance with a minimum of troops and limited material. General Ironside had attempted to contain the advance by adopting the tactics of the First World War and had ordered a series of pillbox designs to be produced. They were to be capable of mounting both British and French weapons and, through commonality of parts, quick to build. These pillboxes were considerably

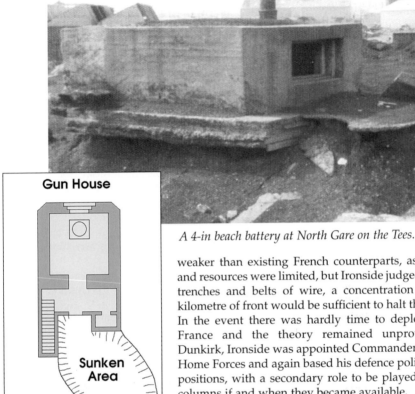

Gun House

Sunken Area

Magazines

A 4-in beach battery at North Gare on the Tees.

weaker than existing French counterparts, as both time and resources were limited, but Ironside judged that, with trenches and belts of wire, a concentration of six per kilometre of front would be sufficient to halt the advance. In the event there was hardly time to deploy them in France and the theory remained unproven. After Dunkirk, Ironside was appointed Commander in Chief of Home Forces and again based his defence policy on fixed positions, with a secondary role to be played by mobile columns if and when they became available.

The main components of this defence was a thick 'Coastal Crust' to frustrate landing, a GHQ Line inland to contain any breakthrough and fortified key tactical areas, or nodal points. Privately, Ironside recognized that, without hope of reinforcement, manning the Coastal Crust would be suicidal and was not unduly upset when he retired in autumn 1940. By October over 14,000 pillboxes had been built but General Brook, his successor, began to overturn this static policy as mobile troops became available. Nevertheless, even when the threat of invasion receded after the Battle of Britain, pillbox construction continued until they were finally banned in 1942. They were erected liberally along the North-East coast, along with emplaced field guns and a number of naval 4-in guns to cover the beaches. These works are beyond the scope of this book but an example of an emplaced 4-in gun is included as an illustration.

Initially, little work was done to improve the existing coast batteries but a large number of 6-in emergency batteries were built from June 1940 onward to

This photograph is thought to have been taken at Seaton Carew emergency battery.

supplement them.

Emergency batteries were makeshift affairs, with many having no more than fifty rounds for each gun. The guns were ex-naval and with their deck mountings only required a simple holdfast and platform. As time allowed, many became more permanent with concrete emplacements, semi-submerged magazines and a whole range of facilities and field defences erected around them. To begin with, many were manned by Marines and Territorials, but the Home Guard took on more responsibility as they gained experience.

The final round of battery building began in 1942. In October 1941 Churchill's attention returned to air defence at a time when new guns were rapidly being manufactured. He requested General Pile to concentrate on mobile forces and efficiency without emplacing more guns which increased manpower requirements. General Pile understood that he could be helped in this task if selected coast batteries could be converted for use in the anti-aircraft role. The weapon of choice was the 5.25-in naval gun but a large number of obsolete 6-in Mk 24 guns were available and these were emplaced instead. Only one site in Britain received the 5.25-in guns, Park Battery at South Shields. It proved inconvenient to convert many existing sites and new three gun batteries were built where it was felt there was a gap in the air defence. Known as Coast Defence Anti Aircraft (CD/AA) batteries they cemented an important development in coast defence as their plotting rooms were linked to radar stations. During 1938 the army had begun working on experimental radars for coast defence and the work was continued by the RAF in the development of the Chain Home Low stations. As well as aircraft they could also monitor shipping and this data could be passed on to a battery plotting room. Further advances led to dedicated coast defence radar sets actually capable of laying guns, which were used very effectively to harass German shipping in the English Channel in 1944.

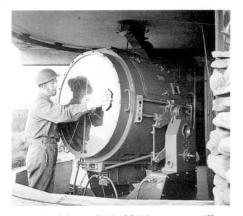

A typical Second World War coast artillery search light.

By 1942 it was clear that the invasion threat was no longer significant and coast defence should be wound down to free men for duty overseas. Apart from the Straits of Dover all counter-bombardment batteries were placed on a care and maintenance basis. Only two close defence 6-in guns and anti-torpedo boat guns, manned by regulars, were to be maintained at each defended port. Emergency batteries were to be manned solely by the Home Guard or go into care and maintenance. The emergency batteries became unviable when Home Guard parades ceased to be compulsory and many batteries were mothballed in 1943, including some of the new CD/AA sites. None, however, was disarmed. Although it is often stated that the emergency batteries were dismantled in 1944, records for this area show that many were reactivated in 1947, at least for a short time.

The following list shows the number of guns at each port at the height of their strength during the war. Also noted are those which were intended to form the backbone of the post-war defences and contain a three-gun CD/AA battery.

Berwick, two 6-in
Amble, two 6-in
Blyth, four 6-in (CD/AA recommended)
Druridge, two 6-in
Tyne, one 9.2-in, three 7.5-in, six 6-in, three 5.25-in, two 12pr (CD/AA implemented)
Sunderland, four 6-in, two 12pr (CD/AA recommended)
Seaham, two 6-in
Hartlepool, four 6-in, two 12pr (CD/AA partially implemented)
Teesmouth, one 9.2-in, two 6-in
Scarborough, two 6-in
Filey, two 6-in
Whitby, two 6-in
Humber, two 9.2-in, seven 6-in, four 4.7-in, two 4-in, six 6pr (CD/AA partially implemented)
Hornsea, two 4.7-in
Grimsby, two 6-in
Mablethorpe, two 6-in

Of particular note are the guns used. Only the pre-war batteries had guns with a calibre above 6-in, except for Frenchman's Fort with its unique 7.5-in guns. Larger guns were of course still being manufactured for the Navy but were rarely used coastal defence during the Second World War.

THE FINAL YEARS

In 1947 the Territorials were reconstituted and the reformed regiments took over their old batteries. Ambitious attempts were undertaken to form new regiments and set up even more batteries, but recruitment among a war-weary population proved unsuccessful. The gunners inherited another problem. Originally the batteries had been fairly small and self-contained but during the war had grown to incorporate a wide range of facilities, often outside the original boundaries. Many of these were now semi-derelict and due for demolition. Accommodation proved a serious problem and many a camp was spoilt by cold and wet nights spent in dilapidated huts. Some work was done to improve matters and morale was boosted by redundant war weapons being issued, in particular the rapid firing twin 6pr and the heavy 3.7-in anti-aircraft gun.

The last major events for the region's gunners took place in 1951. During Hartlepool Charter Celebrations they displayed their prowess to the public in a 'Combined Services Exercise - tracking of an aircraft using radar and searchlights from the shore and naval vessels in the bay. Followed by a Firing practice from the Heugh and Lighthouse Batteries at towed targets.' They also recreated the Bombardment of Hartlepool for the public, although this 'tableau' actually took place at Roker Battery at Sunderland (Hartlepool Charter Celebrations Brochure (Hartlepool Borough Council, 1951): author's collection).

Nevertheless, ammunition remained scarce and complaints were aired by residents, annoyed that guns should be allowed to fire in populated areas. Morale, never high since the end of the war, received a killing blow in 1950 with the introduction of National Service. Accepting that National Servicemen were essential to the batteries' continued survival in the face of poor recruitment, officers were dismayed to find the new men untrained and uninterested in artillery. Even if a man were keen, the fact was that most had ended up at the batteries only as a stop gap before being posted to their proper regiments. After almost one hundred years and two world wars, the tradition of volunteering had all but died out and the batteries had been reduced to little more than transit camps.

Yet the batteries were not quite finished. The perceived threat to Britain now came from Russian planes carrying atomic bombs and, following the usual post-war decline, the Ministry of Defence sought to remedy the situation. Another project was undertaken which, like the Palmerston Forts, was to be the biggest public works programme of its day. In 1951 the wartime radar network was reactivated and large underground bombproof stations built as part of the Rotor programme. These would act primarily to control fighters intercepting the bombers but they could also control the CD/AA batteries. Seventy-one Rotor stations were

A 3.7-in AA gun being used in the coast defence role by 426 Durham Regiment in 1954.

Taken in the last years of coast defence. The gun is a 3.7in AA fitted with Naval sights.

commissioned but CD/AA batteries remained few and far between and the proposed upgrades did not happen. Concerns that AA guns could not match jet aircraft were finally laid to rest with the introduction of the ballistic missile. By the time it was completed in 1955, the Rotor system was obsolete.

Technology had moved on, the old enemies gone and with plans for European integration any future threat to inshore waters removed. The announcement was made on 17 February 1956 by the Minister of Defence and the service ceased on 31 December 1956. The regiments disbanded during October and work to remove the guns and equipment began immediately. The empty batteries, considered by locals as little more than eyesores, were demolished or left to slowly decay. Like their Napoleonic predecessors, they were all but forgotten, their remains serving only as playgrounds for a generation that would finally see peace on the coasts and beaches of Britain.

FAREWELL MESSAGE

On 31st October, 1956, you will be leaving 426 (DURHAM) Coast regiment RA (TA) on disbandment of Coast Artillery. However, I am glad to know that the great majority of you will still be serving on in the Territorial Army.

I would like to take this opportunity of thanking you for all that you have done in the past as Members of a very fine old Regiment RA (TA), and the way you have upheld the traditions and high standards. Many of you are serving on in a new role in a fine Corps, The Royal Engineers, and I want to wish you all the very best of luck in the future in your new role on this sad occasion.

Brigadier, Commander 105 Coast brigade RA (TA).

Edinburgh 26th October, 1956.
(Durham Heavy Brigade Scrapbook, DCRO, D/DLI6/1/6-7)

War Department boundary stones were used to mark battery boundaries. In some cases these are the only surviving relics.

COAST ARTILLERY

MUZZLE LOADING GUNS

The original Victorian batteries in the North-East all mounted smoothbore muzzle loading guns, the ultimate development of gunpowder-firing cannon. At that time new breech loading guns were being developed. In particular, Armstrong had built a successful rifled breech loader at his works in Newcastle in 1854 and by 1861 a 7-in 110pr suitable for coastal defence was ready. It could fire out to about two miles, half a mile further than the 68pr and could be reloaded in slightly less time. Nevertheless, the new guns, ten of which were mounted on HMS *Warrior*, were regarded with suspicion by the Navy as they required gunners with above average training and it was found that the breech block could be blown out if the barrel overheated. Fears were realized in 1863 during the Bombardment of Kagoshima, a dispute with Japan, when twenty-eight accidents occurred during the firing of three hundred and sixty-five rounds. Rather than improve the design or even properly investigate the incident, the Admiralty decided that the breech loader was intrinsically unsafe and muzzle loading was the only viable option. *Warrior's* guns were dismounted and sold to the Confederates during the American Civil War. A small number of these first-generation breech loaders were used in the Palmerston Forts, but none were mounted in the North.

When the Victorians began considering placing guns along the coast they were faced with a virtually blank slate. The earlier Napoleonic batteries had mostly been disarmed and, having been comprised for the most part of little more than simple platforms and earth embankments, had either been demolished or were totally unsuited for mounting the newer guns. The town corporations were quite willing to lease spare land to the War Department, often for little or no rent, but quite often such sites were not particularly suitable and a great deal of work was carried out to lay suitable foundations or slow down the effects of coastal erosion by blocking up crumbling cliffs. Once a site had been chosen the Royal Engineers surveyed and mapped it and a suitable battery was designed within the confines. As it had been found that the most effective way to use guns in warships was to set them in a line and use salvo firing, the same layout was adopted in these early batteries. It was more or less pointless to mount a single gun, as accuracy was at best dubious, and no muzzle loading batteries in the North-East were built for less than two guns.

Two types of emplacement were employed. Within a linear layout the 'V' shaped embrasure sufficed as it was cheap and, although it limited the traverse, this was not a hindrance as only narrow cover was required. Embrasure emplacements were generally built out of brick or whatever local stone was to hand. Where a wider arc of fire was needed, for example at the end of the gunlines, the larger, 'U' shaped barbette emplacement was used, often made of mass concrete. The barbette emplacements also introduced various recesses for the storage of ready to use ammunition, fuses and other equipment required for the guns. Both types were open at the rear so that the gun could be run back for reloading. Battery guns were always numbered, with gun No. 1 being the right-hand gun when viewed from behind the gunline. The only variation to this was when a letter was used to differentiate guns in different batteries, thus H1, H2, S1, S2, would describe two batteries of two guns. Only the guns were numbered, empty emplacements were simply ignored.

The emplacements were joined together by a retaining wall which separated higher ground to the front of the battery and the lower sheltered area behind. This split level arrangement, which gave the batteries a very low profile when viewed from the front, continued in various forms throughout their history. The sheltered area behind, if large enough, was used as a parade and contained barracks and stores.

The guns needed a fairly rapid supply of ammunition and well-protected magazines were built for the high-explosive cartridges. These were often no more than small rooms entered by a shifting lobby where the crew would change into magazine clothes, the entryway being clearly marked by a raised barrier over which they had to step to enter the confines. Magazine regulations were very specific as to what could be taken into the magazine and lamps were never placed inside but stood in a niche in the lobby, and shone through a glass window to cast a dim light on the interior. All lamps used candles, often fitted with a clockwork mechanism to keep the flame level; oil was never used because of the danger of spillage. Within the magazines the cartridges were stored in leather cannisters on wood racks known as skidding and the fuses stored on shelves. Elaborate arrangements for transporting the cartridges to the guns, such as lifts, tend not to be found in the North-East and the magazine crew would simply pass them to a gunner to carry on to the gun. As the smoothbores fired a simple solid iron 'cannon ball', no special storage was needed and they were stacked in pyramids close by the guns, thirty balls in the case of the 68pr.

In the smallest batteries only one building was provided, a side arm store which held the equipment needed to load and traverse the guns and act as a shelter. Larger sites often held a whole range of facilities, such as workshops, the master gunners residence, barrack accommodation for the gunners and cookhouses and food stores.

Unlike the Palmerston Forts, no attempt was made for close quarter defence and simple wooden fences usually marked the perimeter, the only exceptions in

The Lighthouse Battery as an example of a small muzzle loading battery: (1) barbette, (2) embrasure, (3) magazine, (4) side arm store.

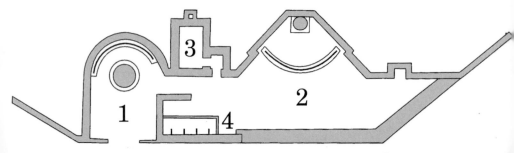

this region being Fort Paull and to a lesser extent the already defensible Tynemouth Castle.

The main batteries were not suited for training as the guns were too expensive to be fired on a regular basis. This, and the fact that the Volunteers were not initially included in the defence plans, led to 'practice batteries' being set up where smaller guns such as the 32pr could be used. They often contained little more than a flat platform for the guns and a wooden hut for shelter and storing side arms. Few survivors have been noted in the North as, along with the huts and rifle ranges also set up on spare ground, they were generally temporary affairs. It should also be remembered that supporting the batteries were external barracks, drill halls and headquarters buildings, many originally built for the Militia in 1860, but these are not covered in this book.

The widespread adoption of the ironclad battleship proved the smoothbore to be utterly inadequate, yet the early breech loaders were considered underpowered, unsafe and, as an 1865 naval committee concluded, 'far inferior to muzzle-loading as regards simplicity of construction and cannot be compared to them in this respect in efficiency for active service.' The Navy determined that the rifled muzzle loader (RML) offered the best compromise. Two schools of thought prevailed at this time, the 'rack fire men' who believed that ever-increasing thicknesses of armour could not be overcome and the best solution was to aim indirect fire onto the decks and literally shake a ship to pieces. Opposing them, 'direct fire men' argued that the only effective method was to punch holes with explosive shells through the armour. Rack fire methods were tested and a number of high angle batteries erected in the South but the method was found unreliable as accuracy was poor and the RML emerged as the only capable weapon. The adoption of the RML was further eased as manufacture was straightforward and, as it was technically simple, there seemed little to go wrong so long as the well-established drill was followed.

For all its power and accuracy, the RML did not gain support in all quarters. The most immediate drawback was the slower loading time, but some of the older veterans voiced more prosaic concerns:

First of all they insisted on having a lot of grooves in the bore of the gun. Now they are only going to have three grooves in the bore of the gun. Please goodness they will next have no grooves at all, and we shall get back to the good old smooth bores which did all that was necessary to beat the Russians and smash the Mutiny.

Another veteran declared that accuracy gave no advantage. On being told that shot from a rifled gun would fall into a much smaller area than that from a smoothbore, he replied that this proved the superiority of the smoothbore: 'With your new-fangled gun firing at me, I have only to keep outside that small area and I shan't be touched. But with a smoothbore firing at me, I'm not safe anywhere!' They may well have had a point: although the rifling conferred much greater accuracy, there was still no means of taking proper advantage of this with a moving target at an undetermined range.

It was highly desirable to be able to convert existing stock rather than design and build a completely new range of guns and the solution was provided by Captain William Palliser of the 18th Hussars. Realizing that the existing weapons were not strong enough to fire the new shells he developed a system whereby the cast iron barrel was drilled out and fitted with a stronger, rifled, wrought iron liner which was then sealed in place by the firing of a heavy proof charge. His system was adopted in 1863 and all guns converted by this method were designated RML. Purpose-built guns were known as MLR (muzzle loading rifled). In all, over 2,000 guns were converted using his system, with the majority carried out at the Royal Gun Factory at Woolwich but several hundred were also contracted out to the Elswick Ordnance Company at Newcastle. As usual the new guns went to the Admiralty first.

Unfortunately, the heavier tighter fitting shell significantly increased loading times and it was found that a short barrel was not effective with the new more powerful brown powders which burnt more slowly. Longer barrels were impracticable as the muzzle had to be easily accessible during loading, which severely limited the mountings that could be used, especially at sea. Such a weapon could be no more than a short-term measure and its days were numbered by the rapid development of new breech loaders.

SMOOTHBORE GUNS

The workhorse of the early batteries was the 68pr, a conventional smoothbore cannon cast from a single piece of iron which would have been recognizable to seamen of earlier generations. It only differed from earlier guns in the size and the mountings used. Although old-fashioned, it was a superb gun for its time and, even though the designer William Dundas was restricted to following existing patterns dating from 1847, it was considered his finest achievement.

In the coast defence role the gun was mounted on a carriage and slide which

68pr smoothbore gun on No. 22 Carriage for use in a barbette emplacement.

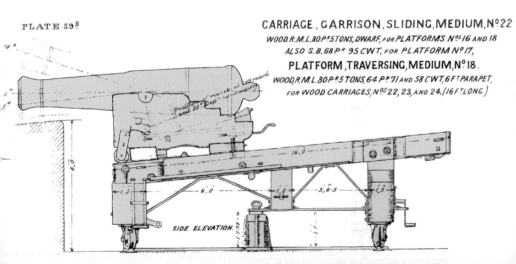

PLATE 59ᴮ

CARRIAGE, GARRISON, SLIDING, MEDIUM, Nº 22
WOOD, R.M.L. 80 Pᴿ 5 TONS, DWARF, ꜰᴏʀ PLATFORMS Nᵒˢ 16 AND 18
ALSO S.B. 68 Pᴿ 95 CWT, ꜰᴏʀ PLATFORM Nº 17,
PLATFORM, TRAVERSING, MEDIUM, Nº 18.
WOOD, R.M.L. 80 Pᴿ 5 TONS, 64 Pᴿ 71 ᴀɴᴅ 58 CWT, 6 FT PARAPET,
ꜰᴏʀ WOOD CARRIAGES, Nᵒˢ 22, 23, ᴀɴᴅ 24, (16 FT LONG.)

SIDE ELEVATION.

allowed the guns to traverse easily within the limits of the emplacement and absorbed the recoil, very necessary as, unrestrained, a 5 ton gun recoiled at a speed of 7 feet per second. Among the ammunition available was the common ball of cast iron for punching through the side of a ship and hollow balls filled with small fragments for use against the crew. The effective range of the 68pr was about a mile and a half, but it was extremely difficult to hit a moving target at this range.

In action, the guns were run back to give the crew access to the muzzle and a black powder charge was rammed home. This was followed by a rope ring, the ball and a second rope ring to hold the round in place. All was then rammed home and the gun run up to fire. A fuse was inserted at the breech end and fired by the No. 1 pulling on a cord. The gun was then run back, sponged out with a wet rammer to extinguish any lingering sparks and reloaded. A well-trained crew could carry this out in fifty-five seconds but it is probably safe to say that the average crew took somewhat over a minute between shots.

RIFLED MUZZLE LOADERS

The replacement for the 68pr smoothbore was the 64pr RML gun, of which two types were adopted, the 64pr of 71 cwt which was converted from the 8-in shell gun and the 64pr of 58 cwt converted from the 32pr of 58 cwt. Several types of ammunition existed for the gun but the most widely used was the common shell. This was of cast iron and about three calibres (16-in) in length with an ogival head. The body held three copper bands with studs to engage the barrel rifling. The shell was hollow, allowing a bursting charge contained in a serge bag to be fitted. Other shells included case shot and shrapnel for use against personnel.

64pr RML gun on No. 23 Carriage. Note how similar both gun and carriage are to the 68pr, enabling the old guns to be upgraded without modification to the existing emplacements.

CARRIAGE GARRISON. SLIDING, MEDIUM, No 23.

SLIDE, L., MEDIUM, No 18.

Scale ⅜ in = 1 Foot.

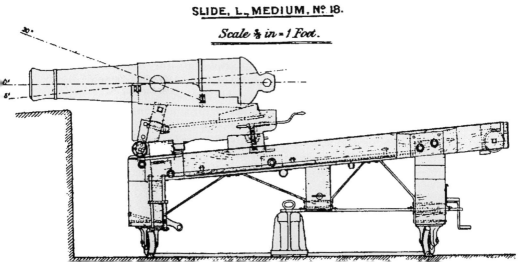

The 64pr RML had a range of 4,000 yards, considerably further than the old 68pr, coupled with the advantages of greater accuracy and an explosive shell. As with the 68pr, the carriage and slide were mostly timber and appear primitive today but this was the preferred material as iron was found to shatter when hit in action, causing terrible injuries. Iron garrison carriages were occasionally used in peacetime, as they required less maintenance, but would be replaced with wood in time of war.

Few modifications were required to the North-East batteries as the RML guns simply dropped into the existing embrasure and barbette emplacements. Shelter for the shells was provided by cutting lockers into the emplacements and retaining wall, preventing the need for alterations to the magazines. The ammunition allowance for each gun remained unchanged as the tight-fitting shell made the new guns slower to load than the smoothbores.

BREECH LOADING GUNS

Developments in the mid-1880s brought about a complete re-evaluation of coastal defence. A new threat arose, that of the lightly armed but fast-moving torpedo boat which could race past a harbour's defences and then, unmolested, wreak havoc. The value of the breech loader had at last been recognized by the Navy and a variety of so-called quick fire guns became available. Other technologies were converging which for the first time would allow proper control of the guns. The telephone gave real time communication to a higher command while the introduction of the rangefinder meant that for the first time guns could be rapidly and accurately laid on to a target.

Warship armament had been divided into two types, the large primary guns for long-range offence and the smaller secondary guns for close defence. The Holy Grail of secondary gun design was the quick firer or QF gun which could smother an enemy vessel in a 'hail of fire'. Originally the design called for the shell to be attached to a metal cartridge case but it was found in practice that, as the calibre increased, it became too heavy and unwieldy. Concern was also expressed about the dangers of storing shell and cartridge together and the idea fell out of favour in Britain for all but the smallest calibres. Another advantage of the shell and bag system was that no elaborate ejection mechanism was required to clear the cartridge after firing, which speeded up the loading process.

For many years Moncrief had pursued the design of the disappearing carriage, where the gun appeared over the parapet only at the moment of firing. His ideas were re-adopted for the new hydro pneumatic (HP) mounting for the 9.2-in and 6-in breech loading guns. The existing emplacements were totally unsuited for conversion and new sites were sought or the existing batteries completely reworked. The new breech loaders were considerably faster firing, which allowed the number of guns at a port to be reduced, but as the ammunition requirement was higher new magazines were also required. The basic design was already

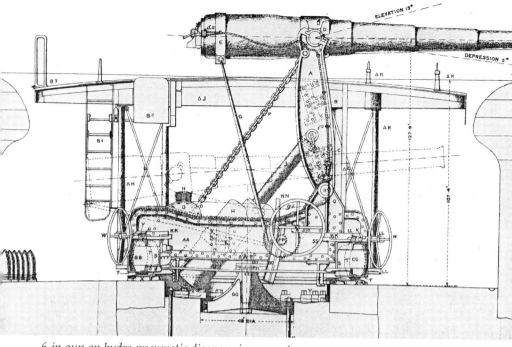

6-in gun on hydro pneumatic disappearing mount.

available as from 1872 Moncrief had also proposed batteries comprising two guns with an underground magazine in-between. He perceived these as powerful self-contained units which could be placed in a dispersed pattern almost anywhere at reasonable cost and replace the existing forts. Initially, the design was controversial, as it challenged financial interests in the heavy iron shields used in casemates, but now they had become obsolete Moncrief's designs were rapidly adopted for the new breech loaders. Also as single guns were now viable, batteries were designed for these for the first time.

The magazine for the HP batteries were invariably placed underground, protected by a concrete roof and substantial sand pad. A flight of steps led down from between the guns to a submerged but open 'courtyard', with several doors leading off to the underground rooms. The magazines were always placed on the seaward side and comprised a shell store illuminated with windows, with the cartridge store running parallel further back. As before, a shifting lobby divided the two and the ammunition stores were also connected by a number of hatches allowing prepared cartridges to be passed through to the lifts in the shell store. Lighting continued to be by candle lamp until the 1930s when electric lighting was introduced, with the shell store acting as a lighting gallery for the cartridge store. In fact, the shell store was considered to be quite safe and in some instances stoves were fitted. The lifts were hand-cranked but could only take ammunition to the surface and davits were provided to fill the magazines. Ventilation was extremely important: thick stone pipes led to Howarth ventilators on the surface.

Often leading off from the submerged 'courtyard' were small lamp rooms and

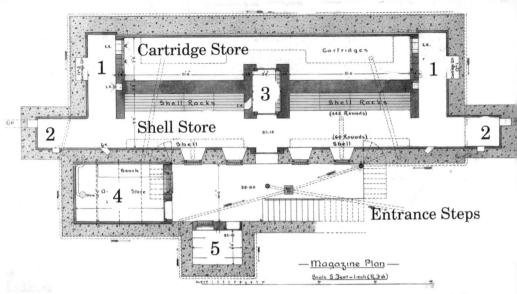

Typical magazine layout showing (1) cartridge lifts, (2) shell lifts, (3) shifting lobby, (4) Royal Artillery store and (5) lamproom.

RA stores where spares for the guns and instruments to align them were kept. Later examples sometimes include a dressing station in the underground section.

When the HP guns were replaced by the central pivot guns there was no need to modify the magazines and the only real difference noted is the dispensing of brick-lined walls and vaulted ceilings.

During the First World War it was realized that the range of coast defence guns must be increased to prevent hostile vessels standing offshore and bombarding towns and commercial targets at their leisure. The first such counter-bombardment guns in the region were mounted at Hartlepool and South Gare in the Palliser and Pasley Batteries where 30 degree mounts were used. This improved the range from eight and a half miles to fourteen and a half miles. With the limitations of the post-war Washington Treaty, the threat to Britain was considered to come from cruisers armed with 8-in guns and the existing 9.2-in guns were considered adequate. The arguments were no doubt reinforced by the fact that to mount the larger naval guns on land would require motors for training and ammunition supply, necessitating a complete rebuild of the works, an expense that was out of the question. Fitting existing 9.2-in and 6-in guns on higher elevation mounts could, with improvements in ammunition, provide a considerable increase in range and it was proposed that this be done throughout the country. Little work was done during the inter-war years and until the Second World War the counter-bombardment role was largely theoretical.

The 6-in gun was also to be used for counter-bombardment on 45 degree mountings but by the time this was carried out in the Second World War the batteries had already been earmarked for dual-purpose Coast Defence/Anti Aircraft defence. A number of these batteries were erected on the North-East coast in 1942 when the approved weapon was the 5.25-in Mk I dual-purpose gun, but 6-in Mk 24 guns were used instead except in Park Battery at South Shields.

HARBOUR DEFENCE GUNS

The first harbour defence guns to be adopted were 3pr QF guns but these were soon found to be too small and were superseded by the Hotchkiss 6pr introduced in 1885. Due to its size only a small holdfast and emplacement was required. In fact, it was so 'portable' that South Gare Battery had alternative emplacements for its guns. Surprisingly, while the HP emplacements afforded both gun and crew the ultimate protection, small QF guns were placed on simple platforms out in the open. A good example of this can be seen at Spanish Battery where the seaward-facing 6-in HP guns were fully protected but the nearby 12pr QF guns covering the Tyne were more or less completely exposed.

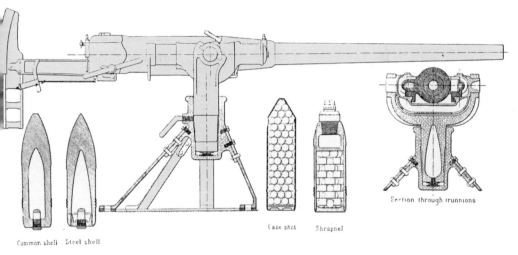

6pr Hotchkiss gun and ammunition. Pistol grips were added after the guns had been emplaced.

The 6pr was widely used in the region and is always associated with submarine mine depots. Nevertheless, when the coast defences were re-evaluated at the turn of the century it was considered too small to be effective and they were removed in 1907. Some of the old stock was reused for sub-calibre training on larger guns and it even made a comeback in 1940 when they were mounted in pillboxes to defend the beaches.

The replacement for the 6pr was the 12pr, an extremely useful weapon which remained in service with little modification from its introduction in 1894 until the end of coast defence. The design of both the gun and its pedestal was quite basic but functional. With no traversing or elevation gear the crew simply pushed and pulled to lay the gun on the target. The No. 1 tracked the target through a telescope and fired using a pistol grip. No ejecting gear was provided until 1935 and the

Typical 12pr emplacement with magazine to left. This is one of a pair overlooking the entrance to the Tyne.

spent cartridge was jerked out with a hand-held hook. Percussion and electrical firing was possible: with the latter, a large lead acid battery was slung under the breech.

The 12pr was equipped with autosights but as it could only be used at short ranges they were not linked to discrete rangefinders. Once the order had been given, the gunners were expected to fire independently.

Most 12pr had been removed by the end of the First World War but many were reinstalled in 1940 as an emergency measure. Nevertheless, the motor torpedo boat, epitomized by the German 'E' boat, was much faster than the earlier torpedo boats and a new weapon was sought from as far back as 1923 and a proposal for a rapid-firing twin-mounted 6pr was made in 1925. Manufacture began in 1933 and, although they were not emplaced in the North-East, some were issued to the region's brigades after the war. It then appears to have been used in a semi-mobile role and for training and kept either at a battery or local drill hall. The twin barrels with semi-automatic breeches gave a rate of fire in excess of 70 rounds per minute and it was very effective against lightly armoured vessels. Although some new gear was required (the Director No. 13), the equipment worked so well that the barrels could be laid independently.

Medium Guns

The 4.7-in gun and above were designated by calibre rather than shell weight, with this gun firing a shell of 45lb weight. It was a superb example of design for its time but its light shell meant that it was never powerful enough as a medium gun. For coast defence it was emplaced but a handful mounted on field carriages were also used. The field version was the local Militia's heaviest and favourite weapon and went on to serve on the Western Front. Introduced in 1888, five marks were produced, on numerous submarks of mounting. All, however, were simple pedestal mounts, apart from the Mk III mount which stood on a pintle for use in 8 foot deep emplacements. With percussion and electric firing, this gun could also be

4.7-in gun

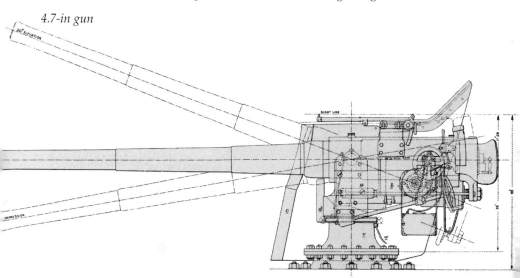

used with a depression rangefinder, but for Case I firing only, unless dials were fitted, as the gun sights had to be used. This was a true QF gun as a brass cartridge case was used. Mk II to IV guns used a three motion breech: that is, three separate operations were required to open or close it. In 1900 the Mk V with a more efficient single motion breech was introduced and the range was increased from 11,800 to 16,500 yards. The early guns were largely withdrawn in the 1920s, although some of the Mk V remained in use, particularly around Humberside. Most of the old emplacements were abandoned as they could not be reworked for larger guns without difficulty.

The 6-in gun firing a 100lb shell was the workhorse of coast defence from 1892 to 1956, although the original guns bear little resemblance to the final versions. The first types introduced to the region were the Mk IV and Mk VI in 1892. They were designed to fire black powder but this was replaced by cordite in the year they were introduced. The barrel and breech weighed 5 tons and it could fire a shell out to 8,000 yards. A three motion breech was used and the cartridges were bags containing 14lb of cordite. As the bag was consumed during firing no extraction mechanism was required, but as there was always the danger of lingering embers in the barrel the breech was swabbed out with water before reloading.

Although barbette and other mounts were available, all the early 6-in guns in the North-East used the hydro pneumatic mount. This was at once eccentric and magnificent, an indirect descendant of Moncrief's original disappearing mount. It was designed so that the gun only appeared above the parapet to fire. Recoil lowered it into the pit for reloading and water pressure then lifted the gun back up over the parapet for another shot. A trial held in 1885 had 'proven' the concept when the guns of HMS *Hercules* failed to hit a mock-up HP mounted gun, but, as Ian Hogg later pointed out, the ship had not only missed the gun but also the emplacement:

> The truth of the matter was that the scientific wizardry of the Royal Carriage Department and Sir William Armstrong, Mitchell and Co. had between them blinded the gunners with science so that they had lost sight of their primary function, which was to shoot at ships and not stare open mouthed as tons of ordnance swung and swooped through the air. The Hercules trial compounded the mischief for in their agreement that the ship had never hit the gun, the observers failed to attach sufficient importance to the fact that it had not been able to hit the emplacement either, and that was not whizzing up and down. (*Coast Defences of England and Wales 1856-1956* (David & Charles, 1974))

The HP mount was developed by Armstrong and Mitchell's Elswick Co. at Newcastle. They were rivals of the Eastern and Anderson Co. that Moncrief had been associated with. It carried an overhead shield to protect the crew from splinters and the gun pit was open at the back to allow penetrating shells an escape route. Although it was rapidly replaced in Britain, the Americans continued to build HP mounts well into the twentieth century. It had one serious limitation. The barrel had to be relatively horizontal, otherwise the forces of recoil were in the

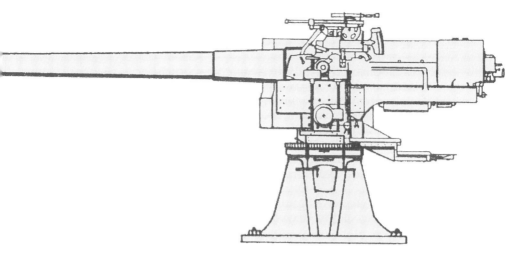

6-in Mk VII on central pivot mount.

wrong direction for the mechanism to work. As elevation was required to increase the range and the mounting was slow in operation it was soon superseded by the simpler central pivot mount.

In 1898 Vickers introduced a new 6-in gun on a central pivot mount. They took advantage of the latest developments to create a very effective design. A more powerful charge was combined with a longer barrel to create a weapon capable of penetrating 22.7 inches of iron as opposed to the 15.9 inches of the 6-in Mk IV. Rate of fire was also improved with a (Welin pure couple) single motion breech, giving a rate of fire of almost 8 rounds per minute. It could fire a high-explosive (Lyddite) or armour-piercing shell out to 12,000 yards on a standard 20 degree mounting. The new gun was introduced in 1901 as the 6-in Mk VII but, having been widely publicized since its inception, it was well known to those involved in coastal defence.

Engineers' drawings of the emplacements often show that they were for QF guns, but the Mk VII was a standard breech loader firing bag charges. A 6-in QF firing brass cartridges was deployed from 1891 but none have been noted in the region apart from the anti-aircraft rail guns of 1915. Following the trend of the earlier harbour defence guns, the Mk VII emplacements offered little in the way of protection to the gun or key members of the crew until 1918, when shields were added to the region's guns. The apparent bulk of the emplacement was due to the solidity of the mount needed for the gun (which was screwed onto 8 foot long bolts embedded in concrete) and also the number of functions it enabled. Lifts served shell and cartridge efficiently to the gun while ammunition was always at hand, stored in ready use lockers. These emplacements were highly standardized and are the most common type to be seen today. Two types were used, one for guns with a traverse greater than 170 degrees and another for guns with a narrower arc of fire. The wide arc emplacements have only one entry way leading to the dials in the gun pit, while the narrow arc emplacements have two. These entrances were originally topped by steel grids to complete the walkway round the gun but these are invariably missing today.

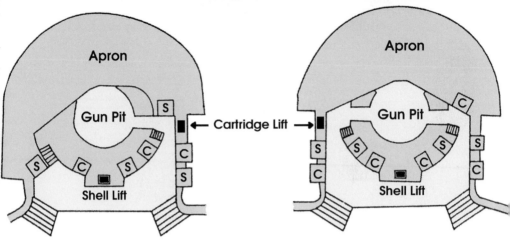

Designs for 6-in Mk VII from the turn of the century with, left, a wide angle and, right, a narrow angle type. C and S indicate the carriage and shell ready use lockers. More variation is found in the wide angle design, particularly in the placement of the steps. These are Heugh No. 2 and No. 1.

The 6-in Mk VII remained in use until coast defence was abolished in 1956. In most batteries the guns were replaced at least once with refurbished ex-naval guns, the old guns being distributed to local drill halls for instructional purposes. Improvements in ammunition over the years extended the range of the 6-in Mk VII considerably. Defying later published sources, the correction tables for Heugh Battery gun H2 show that in April 1942, using a charge of HE XXIXB and CPPBC projectile, a range of 24,000 yards was achieved, the shell being in flight for sixty-nine seconds.

Much effort was put into improving the Mk VII, but with little success as it had been so well designed. The most significant development was a simple, self-levelling naval central pivot mount introduced with the 6-in Mk IX. This did not require an emplacement, merely a simple concrete base, making it ideal for use in the 1940 emergency batteries. A large number of later mark guns were installed in these batteries in the North-East and elsewhere, at first on simple platforms and later in more elaborate emplacements and gun houses. Invariably, as the naval central pivot mount was used in the coast defense role, the guns' elevation and therefore range was limited. The maximum range of the Mk X was about 12,000 yards.

The intention to use 6-in guns in the counter-bombardment role was not carried out here until the introduction of the Mk 24 to land service in 1941. An updated version of the Mk VII with a new breech, it was mounted on a 45 degree high angle mounting. As it was an obsolete naval gun the surplus was used as a stop gap measure, pending the fitting of the new 5.25-in CD/AA guns. The batteries were all designed for three guns, although the full complement was not always fitted. Extensive reworking of emplacements was required when an existing battery was converted as the gun was enclosed in a hydraulically powered turret, requiring a much larger emplacement. A particular example of this was the Lighthouse Battery in Hartlepool where the emplacement was modified from the original 6-in Mk IV

6-in Mk 24 on mount but without turret.

5.25-in CD/AA gun in turret. These guns had a 70 degree elevation.

on HP mount to 6-in Mk VII on CP mount and finally 6-in Mk 24.

The 5.25-in Mk II gun was a true dual-purpose gun with an anti-aircraft range of 43,000 feet and capable of firing proximity fused shells. By 1945, 125 had been released to the army but, apart from those fitted at Park Battery, seem to have been used only in AA batteries in Britain.

The mounting was completely hydraulic powered with elevation traverse and loading powered from an underground engine room. An unconfirmed report states that each mounted gun, complete with emplacement, underground magazine and engine room, cost a quarter of a million pounds.

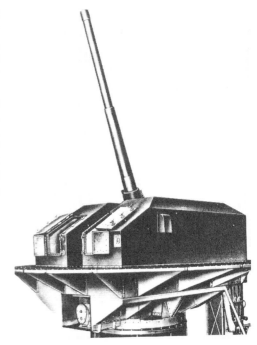

HEAVY GUNS

The 9.2-in calibre gun came about as a result of the Admiralty wanting a gun similar to Krupp's 24 cm gun of 1879 and a number of early types were adopted for coast defence. In 1895 new designs were drawn up, culminating in the Mk X which came into service in 1900. It could fire a 330lb shell out to 25,700 yards on a 30 degree mount and penetrate 14 inches of steel plate at 3,000 yards. The Mk V mount took the form of a high pedestal and the gun fired over a 6 foot 6 inch concrete parapet. A circular steel platform was fitted behind, which served as a walkway round the breech and a 'shell pit shield' for the gunners below. Suspended from this were six trolleys on rails to take ammunition from the shell lifts and then to the breech via hydraulic rams. A davit was also provided to assist manual lifting of ammunition to the breech in case the hydraulics broke down. The breech was single motion and bag cartridges were used. Although better thought of than the subsequent Mk XI, it was known to be inaccurate, especially at certain stages of wear, and had a working life of only 450 rounds before the barrel had to be relined.

When the Hotchkiss 6pr guns were withdrawn in 1907, many were permanently fitted above the 9.2-in barrel to allow sub-calibre ammunition to be used for training.

'Old Bess', the 9.2-in Mk X at Tynemouth Castle. Note the 6pr sub-calibre gun above the barrel.

UNUSUAL GUNS

A number of non-standard guns were employed in the North-East. The most important were the 12-in ex-naval guns used in the Tyne Turrets, the 7.5-in guns at Frenchman's Fort and 4-in guns on the Humber. These are included in the table at the end of this chapter and are described under their respective batteries in the Gazetteer.

After the Second World War, the gunners received a number of ex-aircraft AA 3.7-in guns, along with their associated rangefinders and predictors. These were equipped with naval sights and fixed on makeshift platforms or used as semi-mobile guns. Most of the training was in the coast defence role.

It should also be remembered that the Volunteers received various obsolete weapons, mainly field guns, which did not comprise part of the defences but which could have been pressed into service if required. Even coast guns were issued, with the Hull Volunteers having a 5-in gun at the turn of the century.

HITTING THE TARGET

The early smoothbores were equipped with simple sights, comprising a notch or bar welded onto the barrel or trunnion. As with previous generations, accurate fire was only achieved by watching where the ball fell and trying to make corrections. As a contemporary account states:

> The Number One, after supervising the loading will station himself to windward where he can best observe the strike of the shot, when an enemy ship approached the Fort Commander gave the word and from then on it was every gun for itself. (Hogg, *Coast Defences*)

No special facilities were needed for the gun captain, as his position was determined by the wind and he would move around as necessary to avoid the smoke from the gun. Although ostensibly more accurate and equipped with tangent sights, the laying of the RML guns did not differ significantly and the benefits of accuracy were only really noticeable with static targets against which the gun captain had time to range his shots.

With the increased range of the breech loader, more sophisticated methods were required. Colonel Watkins provided a solution in 1885 with his depression range finder (DRF), which could accurately determine the range by tracking a target through a telescope. These were fitted in purpose-built posts containing a deeply sunk concrete pillar to dampen vibration. Early versions could only determine range but the ability to calculate bearing was soon introduced. Watkins improved it further and brought out the position finder (PF) with which a target's position could be plotted on a chart and converted into data for a number of guns. Further enhancements allowed a moving target's future position to be calculated, a major breakthrough as a 6-in shell fired out to 15,000 yards was in the air for thirty seconds.

Initially, the data for the guns were passed verbally to the gunners by the fire commander, often assisted by a megaphone, but this was soon superseded by electrically connected dials at the rangefinder and near the guns. The fire commander applied any corrections he thought necessary and set the range and bearing on a pair of dials at the rangefinder which were transmitted to the battery commander's 'read-only' dials. He could then apply any further corrections for individual guns before shouting them across and ordering fire. Finally, dials were placed in the gun pit and all the gunner had to do was ensure that the data needle was lined up with the gun position needle as he rotated the gun. A system of alarms and gongs was set up to control the guns. Order gongs provided the open fire signal and the fire commander had a 'gun ready signal lamp' on his control panel. Bells were used to pass on general orders such as cease fire or stand down.

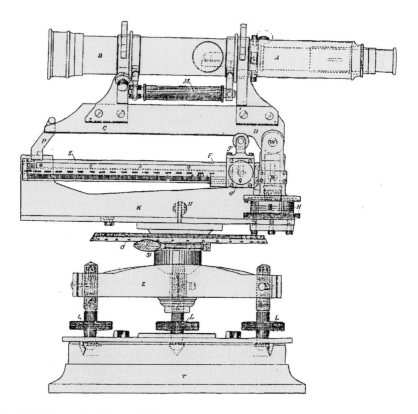

Mark II* Depression Range Finder

For the first time the gun could be laid even if the crew could not see the target, with the added advantage that the instrument and guns could be located in the best position for their purpose.

The Watkins DRF and PF had one disadvantage: they relied on being a known height above a fixed-base level and this was affected by the tide. Compensation, by calibrating on a known target such as a feature in the landscape had to be made and large calibration boards, divided into four black and white squares, appeared at various points along the coast. Later, floating buoys and even lorries were used as calibration aids, with the pattern painted on their sides. The setting up of the guns went as follows:

Following morning parade the crews were detailed to their respective guns. The gunlayer adjusted the telescopes elevation and traverse. The No. 2 inspected the breech and made sure the firing lock was available. The No. 4 made sure the ramrod and bucket were in order and the loading numbers checked the ready use lockers. The gun No. 1 then

Heugh Battery command post for a depression rangefinder dating from 1914. The brick rooms behind are the telephone room and meat store.

proceeded to check the gun using a clinometer taking into account the height above sea level, average mean tide and barometric pressure. When this was all worked out it was applied to the clinometer and placed on the clinoplane above the breech. The gun then had to be traversed on to a datum board and the elevation gun layer aligned his sight. Communications between the Battery Observation Post and the gun were then tested. When the No. 1 was satisfied that all was correct he reported to the officer of the watch 'No. 1 gun correct and crew closed up'. In the event of a break in communications between the BOP and gun the No. 1 took over and directed fire from outside the gun shield using an open sight fastened to the side. (Stockill letters, author's correspondence and interview)

The Watkins DPF was not only used to direct guns but was also found to be the ideal way of firing submarine mines. As the target's track was drawn on the chart it was easy to identify which mine it was passing over and mechanical switching was added to automatically connect the required mine to the firing block.

A variant of the depression position finder was the horizontal position finder. This was used where a site was not high enough above sea level to give an accurate reading and a horizontal rather than vertical measurement was made by using two observing stations, one known as the transmitter and the other the receiver. The transmitter (or transmitting cell) sited furthest from the guns comprised of little more than a telescope, while the receiver, close to the guns, was more or less a complete DRF complete with electric dials. The bearing of the transmitter telescope was relayed by cable to the receiver and used to calculate the range and bearing of the target, which was then transmitted to the battery.

The Navy, using larger guns at extreme range, needed an instrument with greater accuracy than the DRF. They sponsored a competition to develop a rangefinder capable of an accuracy of 3 per cent at a distance of 3,000 yards, which was jointly won in 1891 by Professors Barr and Stroud of Glasgow University and the Yorkshire College. The resultant Barr and Stroud rangefinder contained two low-power telescopes in a tube to give a stereoscopic image, which when focused by the operator gave the range on a scale in the eyepiece. It required little training and under normal conditions could be operated in under twelve seconds. Unlike the Watkins rangefinder it was easily calibrated and required no compensation for the tide. The Barr and Stroud was rapidly adopted by the Navy but not by coast artillery until the introduction of the fortress plotting system. Accuracy was dependent on the length of the optic tube and types used in the North-East varied between 9 and 30 feet. The Barr and Stroud, along with the DRF, remained in service until the end of coast defence.

A Barr and Stroud rangefinder from 1907. When used in the batteries they were fitted in lightly armoured turrets.

A director being used to control a 3.7-in coast gun. These mechanical computers could calculate corrections from elevation and bearing data but were not used with the larger guns in the region.

To take advantage of a rangefinder it was necessary that the time between ranging and firing be reduced to a minimum and, even when the position finder was used to extrapolate the future position, the gun still had to go off at the right moment. As breech loaders were capable of electrical firing they were connected to a firing plug placed close to a set of dials and the firing gong under the control of the gun captain or battery commander. Using this method, a pair of guns could be fired simultaneously by one man. It was even possible to place the firing block under the control of the fire commander.

All guns have an intrinsic accuracy which changes as the barrel wears. A periodic calibration was essential and the results were carefully compiled and kept in the fort record book. This gave corrections for drift caused by the rifling, temperature, atmospheric pressure and wind, as well as firing different projectiles. With this the commander could make corrections for individual guns to the rangefinder data. He needed good mental arithmetic but with enough practice and watching the fall of shot it probably become quite intuitive. Calibration was carried out when the guns were fitted and then occasionally after that. It was always a memorable event for the gunners as it gave them the opportunity to fire at least ten full charge rounds from one of their own guns.

Case I, II, III

Three methods of controlling the guns by rangefinder were developed, known as Case I, Case II and Case III. These techniques were used throughout the life of the breech loading batteries.

Case I was the simplest method of using a rangefinder. The gunner used the gun sights to lay for both line and elevation, having been informed of the range to the target. Case I was rarely used as there was the problem of error when judging the elevation on the gun sight, particularly at night. Either a DRF or position finder could be used.

In Case II the gunner laid the gun for line. The rangefinder crew found the range and applied corrections to a dial at the rangefinder post. This was transmitted either to the battery commander who made further corrections for each gun in his charge or directly to a dial under the gun. A second gunner (who was unable to see the target) read the gun dial and set the correct elevation from under the gun. Case II was widely practised and was often the preferred method. Again either a DRF or position finder was suitable.

Case III was similar to Case II, except that laying for line was calculated by a position finder and transmitted to a second dial under the gun, and the gun sights were not used. With the introduction of the fortress plotting system this became the preferred method, although corrections were then calculated at the battery plotting room. Later Case III became synonymous with radar control. There is no evidence for directors, mechanical computers to calculate corrections, being used for coast guns in the North-East. Had Case III been combined with a director and electrical firing, the result would have been the ability to fire completely by remote control.

To sum up, in Case I laying was done using the gun sights, in Case II one sight was used to point the gun at the target and in Case III the gun sights were not used at all.

Autosights

Anti-torpedo boat guns such as the 12pr could not be used effectively with a discrete rangefinder as the gun was manually brought to bear on the target. The need for rapid and accurate laying led to the development of the autosight. The principles were similar to the DRF but using a pair of sights for line and elevation, fitted to the gun carriage. It proved suitable on guns up to 6-in calibre for occasions when the rangefinder was out of action or if there were multiple targets, as most rangefinders could only track one at a time. Unfortunately, it could only be used at short ranges, this being dependent on the height of the gun and size of target. For example, the autosights at the Heugh Battery were usable against a battleship at 4,256 yards and a smaller destroyer at 2,550 yards. As with the DRF, the gun had to be calibrated against a known target to take the tide into account and compensation was made by adjusting gearing in the elevating mechanism.

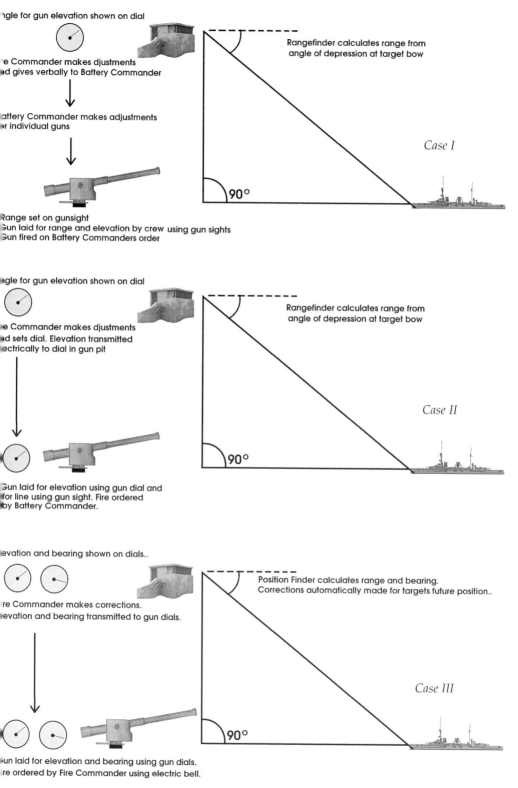

gle for gun elevation shown on dial

e Commander makes djustments
d gives verbally to Battery Commander

attery Commander makes adjustments
r individual guns

Range set on gunsight
Gun laid for range and elevation by crew using gun sights
Gun fired on Battery Commanders order

Rangefinder calculates range from
angle of depression at target bow

90°

Case I

gle for gun elevation shown on dial

e Commander makes djustments
d sets dial. Elevation transmitted
ectrically to dial in gun pit

Gun laid for elevation using gun dial and
for line using gun sight. Fire ordered
by Battery Commander.

Rangefinder calculates range from
angle of depression at target bow

90°

Case II

evation and bearing shown on dials..

re Commander makes corrections.
evation and bearing transmitted to gun dials.

Gun laid for elevation and bearing using gun dials.
re ordered by Fire Commander using electric bell.

Position Finder calculates range and bearing.
Corrections automatically made for targets future position..

90°

Case III

THE FORTRESS PLOTTING SYSTEM

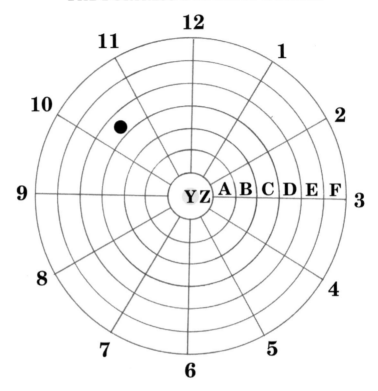

Observers used the 'clock code' to report fall of shot. Here the rounds are overshooting to the left at 10 o'clock D. This was reported to the battery plotting room who would convert it into range and bearing corrections for the guns.

With the intention to mount guns for counter-bombardment came the problem of extreme range. The proposed fortress at Singapore was to be fitted with 15-in guns and it was imperative to be able to use them at their furthest reach. Experimental techniques in 1930 involved salvo firing with the fall of shot being observed by aircraft and transmitted back by radio to a fortress plotter who converted the corrections into elevation and bearing for the guns. The simple charts of the position finders gave way to large peg board plotting tables showing target position and fall of shot. Unlike the RAF plotting rooms, where markers were elegantly swept around, croupier style, the pegs were popped through holes by men under the table! By 1934 the system was formalized with the introduction of the fortress plotting system. This required discrete fortress observation posts, together with fortress and battery plotting rooms, and its working is well described in the Durham Heavy Brigade's Digest of Service for 1935:

Included in a full series of practice was a series fired by an improvisation of the Fortress Plotting System, the ranges and bearings from two flank observation posts being passed by telephone to a Fortress Plotting Room and there converted into coordinates and passed by telephone to a Battery Plotting Room, whence they were converted into gun range and bearing and passed by electric dials to the 9.2-in gun.

Improvisation was the key word, as no plotting rooms existed at this time and and many drill halls were hastily adopted for practice. In fact, much of the pre-war training took place using either sub-calibre ammunition or mobile 6pr guns. It became the preferred way of controlling the guns as the fortress commander could now see the whole picture and coordinate all the guns under his command. The Second World War provided the boost needed to get the system implemented and 1940 saw the building of the plotting rooms. One weakness of the system, the vulnerability of the telephone lines, was soon overcome with the introduction of wireless sets and many old telephone rooms in the batteries were converted for wireless sets. Two sets are known to have been used in the North-East, the WS no. 9 and no. 18. The no. 9 came into service in 1939 as a tank set and had a range of thirty-five miles with both morse and speech (CW and RT). The no. 18 dating from 1940 had a shorter range of only ten miles and was portable. Each battery was equipped with one set, while the fortress command posts were fitted with banks of each, as the no. 9 and no. 18 sets operated on different frequencies.

The original battery command posts gave way to more substantial battery observation posts and during the Second World War each fort was equipped with a number, often in multi-storey blocks or at the base of steel lattice towers. Hartlepool, with only two 6-in guns and two 12pr, had by 1943 a 9 foot Barr and Stroud, three DRF, a four-storey close defence battery observation post, a steel tower with 18 foot Barr and Stroud on top and two counter-bombardment observation posts, all under the control of a fortress command post on the Tees.

This new infrastructure paved the way for the next technological stride which would allow the batteries to engage targets that could not be seen from the shore.

The fortress plotting system using Case III radar.

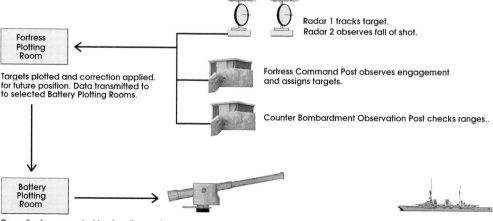

Radar 1 tracks target.
Radar 2 observes fall of shot.

Fortress Plotting Room

Targets plotted and correction applied. for future position. Data transmitted to to selected Battery Plotting Rooms.

Fortress Command Post observes engagement and assigns targets.

Counter Bombardment Observation Post checks ranges..

Battery Plotting Room

Co-ordinates converted to elevation and bearing for individual guns.

In June 1939 Churchill was to write:

The progress in RDF especially applied to rangefinding must surely be of high consequence to the Navy. It would give power to engage an enemy irrespective of visibility. How different would have been the fate of the German battlecruisers when they attacked Scarborough and Hartlepool in 1914 if we could have pierced the mist. (*The Second World War*, vol. 2, *Their Finest Hour* (Cassell & Co., 1949)

Radio direction finding or radar stations were set up along the South and East coasts from 1936 on, with the intention of detecting enemy aircraft. However, it was also noted that they could monitor shipping and, with the introduction of Chain Home Low (CHL) radar, some accuracy could be achieved. A number of these stations were designated CHL/CD (coast defence) and monitored both the sky and sea. Data was sent directly to the local fortress plotting room which then controlled the guns using the existing fortress plotting system. It was found that not only could vessels be tracked but the fall of shot could also be seen and corrections duly made. With the development of the cavity magnetron portable ultra high frequency sets with extremely good resolution became possible and by September 1940 sets were being made to control AA guns and searchlights. Similar work was carried out by the Navy and derivations of these sets were used to control coast guns. Two sets were used, one to track the target and the other to observe the fall of shot. Although a number of the CHL/CD stations have been identified in this area, no details of the smaller sets have come to light, although it is likely that they were installed in or quite close to the batteries. Radar-controlled coast guns proved very useful when they were used to attack German shipping hugging the French coastline at night and a number of sinkings were reported. When the batteries closed in 1943 the radar sets were removed, so that in the 1950s the North-East batteries became dependent on the CHL/CD stations again. Those stations which have been identified are:

Kinley Hill CHL, near Seaham feeding battery plotting room at Heugh Battery

Saltburn (probably naval 10 cm coastwatching sets), reporting to Tees fire command and Newcastle fortress plotting rooms

Goldsborough CHL and naval 10 cm coastwatching sets, feeding Whitby Battery plotting room

Ravenscar (probably naval 10 cm coastwatching sets), reporting to Newcastle fortress plotting room

Bempton CHL and naval 10 cm coastwatching sets, feeding Filey Battery plotting room

Second World War close defence battery observation point, at Lighthouse Battery. To the left is the old BCP (as shown on p.25) and the row of houses to which the proposed BCP on p.36 was to have been attached.

SEARCHLIGHTS

To protect a harbour mouth from night attack and assist the examination service in its normal duties, it became apparent that some form of illumination was necessary. Experiments were carried out between 1879 and 1887 and the electric arc lamp was found to be most suitable, which with a 3 degree 'pencil' beam had a range out to about one mile. When they were first installed, difficulties were found in tracking a moving target with such a narrow beam and this was gradually widened. Known as defence electric lights (DEL) they were initially used to cover submarine minefields and to assist the examination gun. Electricity was supplied from underground engine rooms. In the early days these contained dynamos powered by steam engines and incorporated a coal store and external watertank. Later the lights could be powered from the local mains supply but all had a back up in the form of diesel generators, again placed in engine rooms. By the First World War the rotating 3 degree beam had been reintroduced, while fixed wide beams were used to illuminate examination areas.

An unusual form of light was used at Fort Paull on the Humber. It comprised a

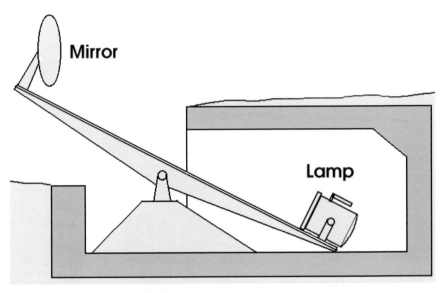

Fort Paull 'see-saw' searchlight.

'see-saw', with the lamp at one end and a mirror on the other. The lamp was protected by a roofed emplacement and shone into the mirror, which when raised above the roof illuminated the required area. Obviously the mirror was the most vulnerable part of the setup but it is not known if spares were kept to repair damage sustained in action. Thought to date from 1886, the only other known example of this type is at Fort Victoria on the Isle of Wight.

Although fixed lights only required turning on, groups of narrow beam lamps required controlling to keep on target. This was done by a Royal Engineers officer from a director's post, and many were built in the region in 1907.

During the Second World War virtually all 6-in batteries were equipped with one narrow beam coast artillery search light (CASL) per gun, often under remote control. Shortages meant that the emergency batteries were often equipped with converted AA searchlights but all types were enclosed in 'D' shaped steel shuttered concrete emplacements. All coast defence lamps were used exclusively for anti-ship use and could not be elevated for use in an anti-aircraft role.

Royal Engineers DEL director's post built in 1907 at Fort Paull.

TABLE OF BREECH LOADING GUNS
USED IN NE DEFENCES

Gun type	Calibre/ shell weight	Introd.	Range	Rate of fire	Comments
Harbour Defence					
3pr QF Hotchkiss	1.85-in	1885	4,000	25 rpm	Sub-calibre use in NE
6pr QF Hotchkiss	2.24-in	1885	7,500	20 rpm	
12pr QF	3-in	1894	7,000	15 rpm	
6pr Twin	3-in	1940	6,200	70 rpm	Practice use in NE
Medium					
4-in Mk 5	25lb	1887	7,700	8-10 rpm	WW2 beach defence
4-in QF Mk V	31lb	1915	9,000	10-15 rpm	Humber Forts
4.7-in	45lb	1888	11,800	5-6 rpm	
5-in	43lb	1890	10,500	10 rpm	Volunt. practice gun
6-in Mk IV	100lb	1885	10,000	3-4 rpm	
6-in Mk VII	100lb	1899	12,000	5-7 rpm	
6-in Mk 24	112lb	1933	25,480	6-8 rpm	CD/AA
5.25-in	80lb	1940	23,400	7-10 rpm	Park Battery CD/AA
Heavy					
7.5-in Mk VI	200lb	1919	15,000	5-6 rpm	Frenchman's Fort
9.2-in Mk III	380lb	1881	11,430	1 rpm	HP gun
9.2-in Mk X	380lb	1900	15,500	3-4 rpm	
9.2-in Mk X HA	380lb		29,200	3-4 rpm	
12-in Mk VIII	850lb	1895	14,860	0.5 rpm	Tyne Turrets

Year of introduction is when they were formally accepted by the Navy. Range and rate of fire should be read with caution as many variables are involved. Range quoted (in yards) is for the gun at introduction on standard coast defence mounts, but this could be varied by the size of charge and later more aerodynamic shells. Rate of fire is dependent on the crew's ability, the mounting and conditions they were operating under, and excludes breakdowns and the 'fog of war'. Calculating an average for the Heugh guns during the Bombardment of Hartlepool gives the 6-in Mk VII a rate of fire of only 2.5 rounds per minute.

GUNNERS

VICTORIAN REGULARS, MILITIA AND VOLUNTEERS

For most of the time the batteries were empty. Only during the First and Second World Wars were they manned on anything like a full-time basis. Occasionally, when the army was mobilized, they were activated and some of the larger sites played host to summer camps and weekend training sessions. Regular soldiers were employed for administration and maintenance and were based at Tynemouth Castle and Fort Paull, where barracks, offices and other facilities were in place. These were the only sites in the region which were occupied permanently.

The Coast Brigades were formed in 1859 and divided into ten divisions to cover England, Scotland and Ireland. The 1st Tynemouth Division was responsible for all the defences in the region and their numbers slowly grew to match the new works. They operated from Tynemouth Castle and were accommodated in the barracks or at Cliffords Fort. A small number were distributed to the other ports and accommodated at the main battery. By way of example, in 1881 two men of the Coast Brigade were living at the Heugh Battery: Corporal Thomas Mc Neill, a 41-year-old Irishman, assisted by Gunner William Wright, aged 34 from Essex. They were each provided with a room in the main battery building and had a small allotment. Entertainment could be had either in the town or in the Militia barracks, where they could play billiards, a favourite pastime for the artilleryman. Married men and their families generally resided at Tynemouth, where more suitable accommodation was available. Fortunately, as time went on and the burden of work grew, married quarters were built in other parts of the region, allowing a fairer distribution of master gunners. An impression of life in married quarters can be gathered from Ethel Hunt's visit to Fort Paull which she later recalled in a letter:

What a place, a big bare room, a fireplace and on one side, a cupboard in the corner. No sink, no water. No nothing in this room . . . I made a rude remark and my escort said he hadn't finished yet, there was more. Every morning the Duty Officer came in on his rounds, entered all quarters and pushed his snooty nose in every corner and with his swagger stick (in case he got contaminated) lifted up the bedclothes. All breakages and damages was entered into his note book.

In 1891 the Coast Brigades were abolished and replaced by the District Establishments. The arrival of the breech loading batteries increased the work they had to undertake dramatically. Not only were the new guns more complex but the new rangefinders also needed calibrating and maintaining. On top of this they also found themselves having to train the part-time gunners on the new equipment. Their officers, seconded from the Royal Artillery, not only had to organize and oversee this work but also found themselves increasingly involved in the

Watercolour showing Militia uniforms in 1878.

administration of the part-time forces, even to the extent of arranging balls and social functions.

For many years it was unclear who would actually man the batteries. Nominally they would be drawn from the Militia Corps, but a second force, the Volunteers, spent many years waiting in the wings.

The Militia were raised before the batteries were built so their number and disposition bore no relevance to the defences they might be expected to man. To begin with, this was not a problem as they were simply a force to be drawn on and they were expected to be able to handle coast defence guns as easily as field guns. As this remained the official attitude for many years, 'batteries' of men were not assigned to 'batteries' on the ground, rather a corps might be assigned to defences in their area when required. The Militia were at first largely recruited from the

1906 Militia recruitment poster.

working class and led by the old aristocracy, the former tending towards violent disturbance and the latter incompetence. Their very existence angered many Royal Artillery officers who had to undergo two years' training and study before earning their commission, which they now saw being handed out indiscriminately to the Militia. They had a valid point: out of the twenty-eight corps raised in 1855 only seven had a commanding officer who had actually served with the Royal Artillery.

As reforms were put in place, the Militia became more efficient and professional. In 1892 Britain experienced a series of major strikes and the Militia were dispatched to keep order. A reputation for violence preceded them but this was a different generation of men who now carried out their duties more by persuasion than force. An enlightened government was eager to avoid bloodshed and public concern was alleviated by knowing that the Militia were no longer a force to be unleashed on them in times of disruption.

Nevertheless, the Militia were never properly prepared, with each man spending only three to four weeks at camp where he received any instruction. There he would spend an hour in the morning drilling and the afternoon learning about artillery. If lucky, he might be involved in firing one of the ninety rounds allocated to his battery that year. Rarely was this training done at the local batteries and the Durham and North Yorkshire men often found themselves training on field guns at their depot in Scarborough, a town with no coast guns at all.

The Militia artillery were liable to be called up and sent abroad in times of war

Durham RGA at Southsea camp 1906. Note they are still armed with Martini Henry single shot rifles.

and were embodied four times. For the Crimean War, the Indian Mutiny and the threat of war with Egypt in 1882, their services were not required, but local men were sent abroad during the Boer War. A service company was made up of men from six corps, including the Durham Militia Artillery. Sent to Durban they formed a unit called the Durham and Edinburgh RGA under Colonel H P Ditmas of the Durham RGA. An account of their part in the battle at Fort Prospect was published by their commander, Captain Rowley of the Dorsetshire Regiment, in the *London Gazette* in December 1901.

At about 4:30am under the cover of mist in the donga, the Boers made a very severe attack on the north and west of my position, the brunt of the attack fell on two sangers held by the Durham Company of Artillery; the Boers broke through the wire and got to within twenty yards of these sangers, but they both gallantly held their own, and I, with the aid of the Maxim was able to repulse this attack. . . . The Boers now had completely surrounded the camp, but contented themselves by keeping up a heavy fire chiefly directed at the Maxim Fort. This fire was kept up all day, gradually lessening towards evening, when the Boers drew off about 6:30pm.

Casualties were light, with only six men slightly wounded, but their behaviour under fire led to a number of them being mentioned in dispatches and recommended for medals, although none were given.

While they were away, their comrades had been called on to man the coast

Officers of the Durham Militia, with Colonel H P Ditmas on the left.

Durham RGA Militia at Southsea 1906, firing the 4.7-in field gun.

defences but had shown themselves unsuited to the task. Their lack of training, coupled with the increasing complexity of coast defence, was a serious cause for concern. Indeed, the validity of all the Militia forces was coming under scrutiny, particularly as the Volunteers were proving themselves a more capable force.

I do not intend any bias against the Militia, but there is a dearth of information on their activities. As the Volunteers were the direct ancestors of the Territorials and caught the public interest, it is their records which tend to have been preserved. There is no doubt that the Militia improved over the years and some officers such as Moncrief were both inventive and capable of informing future opinion. It was in fact the enthusiasm and hard common sense of one Militia officer that led the British army into the air. Lieutenant J. Temple set up a ballooning school in the Royal Engineers, the forerunner of the Air Battalion, Royal Flying Corps and ultimately the RAF. Overcoming numerous difficulties, he was able to prove that aerial observation and photography would be invaluable for directing artillery fire. One can only guess at the thoughts of the local gunners when they saw the first balloons working at the Lydd practice camp in 1886.

In the wake of the Crimean War a burgeoning, business-oriented and educated middle class began to question the competence of the old aristocracy. The technological developments of the war had been driven by business interests and they now felt qualified to extend their sphere of influence. The situation was aptly summed up by a little ditty published in Punch in 1855.

No more will we be ruled by men
Whose sole qualification
Is not ability and ken;
But lies in rank and station:
None shall this land
Henceforth command
No men will we submit to,
But those who business understand;
Practical men of ditto.

Wishing to prove themselves, local worthies loudly advocated the Volunteer corps and formed themselves into an officer corps. The Hull Volunteer Artillery was commanded for its first months by Major Zachariah Pearson, better known as the Mayor.

Honorary colonels, invariably the lord lieutenants of the county, provided financial assistance to the corps, their subscription being set at £100 per year. Other officers also paid subscriptions in line with their rank, lieutenant colonels £50, majors £40, captains £30 and lieutenants £20. Non-commissioned officers also had a sliding scale from sergeant majors at 30 shillings to sergeants at 16 shillings and other ranks paying 10 shillings. It is not surprising that among the founding officers we find stockbrokers, solicitors and entrepreneurs and from time to time they were expected to fund various purchases out of their own pockets. Given that one of the Volunteers' supposed aspirations was to replace 'the aristocracy's private army', the Militia, it is notable that Lord Londonderry's estate managers were all expected to enrol in the Seaham Volunteers as officers, regardless of suitability.

Initial fundraising efforts highlight the social standing of this new officer corps. A plethora of balls were planned and even special trains laid on to ferry the guests back and forth. Their part in the civic hierarchy was underscored by numerous public events and their providing guards of honour for notable visitors. Bands were formed immediately and paraded at every opportunity.

The Volunteers were formed as 'clubs' who then offered their services to the War Office. Their independence was reflected in the freedom to design their own uniforms and they adopted the standard Royal Artillery uniform with white facings and silver braid instead of red and gold. Officers of course bought their own and while they were finely arrayed the lower ranks were less well catered for. A uniform suitable for marching was worn but working clothes were scarce and proper clothing for operating the guns was not introduced until 1881. When training informally at weekends it was quite common for the men to wear their own clothes.

In 1862 the War Office invited the Volunteers to introduce camps for training but extra funding was not offered and few took place. This was followed by an order that each volunteer must attend an annual inspection parade to be considered efficient. This was considered 'inconvenient' by some officers, particularly as the annual government grant was dependent on the number of 'efficients' in a corps. Officers grudgingly realized that they were expected to work for their position. The War Office issued the first set of regulations for the new corps in 1863 and at last the Volunteers began to adopt a more professional attitude, with fines introduced for officers who failed to attend meetings. Hull must have had particular problems with their 'inefficients' as the town's pawn shops were instructed that it was illegal to take in uniforms and other corps equipment.

Far more serious was the occasional rogue officer. A disagreement in Hull sparked a situation verging on the mutinous in 1878. Captain Yates was the adjutant, a full-time Royal Artilleryman, carrying out administrative duties for the corps. When he became aware of financial irregularities he declared that he could

Colonel Humphrey, CO 2nd East Riding RGA Volunteers, 1873 to 1880.

no longer work for the Volunteer commanding officer and resigned. Captain Yates was an able officer and soon received promotion to major. His allegations were passed on to the Secretary of State for War for consideration. Colonel Humphrey, the Volunteer CO, suffered the indignity of having his fate revealed in the House of Commons. The Secretary of State for War declared that Humphrey's resignation would not be enforced 'if a properly qualified Adjutant was willing to accept a position under him'. Such a man could not be found immediately and Humphrey remained the head of the corps. At the same time a group of officers had hired High Paull House for their entertainment, which gave them the ideal venue to discuss the shortcomings of their commanding officer in private.

Humphrey tried to deflect the mounting criticism by calling a special parade so all could hear where the money had been spent. He revealed that £2,000 had been borrowed but this was being spent on setting up the new barracks. The officers remained unconvinced and, following 'grave dissention', brought a formal complaint leading to a Court of Enquiry. The trial was an embarrassment and the charges were declared 'unsupported' and 'frivolous', leaving the officers incensed and causing four to resign. Privately, the court recognized that the charges had some foundation and discreetly gave Humphrey only one option, to resign. He was not a man to go down without a fight and appealed, only to be officially informed by the War Office that his retirement was indeed required. Humphrey smouldered for a month before taking action and

> caused postcards to be sent to every member, earnestly requesting them, as a personal favour to himself, to meet him in plain clothes at the barracks, when he intended making a most important statement affecting the interests of the whole Brigade. (R. Saunders, *History of 2nd East Riding of Yorkshire Royal Garrison Artillery Volunteers*, Hull (Walker & Brown, 1907))

Over 800 men attended, where they heard a 'pathetic farewell' as Humphrey announced his forthcoming resignation. He was then followed by Captain Thorpe, who made a speech in his favour and, backed up by Captains Wellesley and Sharp, called on the men to resign en masse. Thirty men walked out in disgust but a resolution of censure against the War Office was actually passed. The War Office were quick to act against a 'resolution so subservient of discipline' and 'calculated to induce a spirit of insubordination'. They ordered a special parade to be attended by the full corps and many of the region's senior officers. There, very publicly and without prior warning, the immediate removal of Humphrey, Thorpe, Wellesley, Sharp and two senior NCOs from the corps was announced.

Regardless of scandals among the officers, the Volunteers' proficiency increased markedly as time went by. In the early years they rarely had the resources to practise on artillery but carbine shooting competitions were held from the start. A good example took place in May 1865 at the rifle range in West Hartlepool where the competitors had to fire five rounds at targets between 100 and 300 yards away. There were five prizes, each named after the sponsor, the last of which was donated by the battery sergeant major:

1. The Tradesmans Prize, a silver cup worth three pounds
2. The Licensed Victuallers Prize, a gold albert
3. The Ladies Prize, a timepiece
4. Mr Hills Prize, opera glasses
5. Sgt Major Scailes Prize, a photographic portrait of the winner

Only men of 4th Durham Volunteer Artillery were allowed to compete. Shooting was with the regulation artillery carbine, a cut-down version of the muzzle loading Enfield rifle. Appropriate military behaviour was expected:

Sgt T Oates of Tyne Submarine Miners in 1893 with medals and prizes won for shooting the Martini Henry.

The squad will fall-in two deep at one o'clock and load from the word of command only, and not to cap before marching out to fire, no talking in the ranks allowed. Anyone infringing the same will be find 2s 6d or expelled from firm. Each competitor will provide own ammunition. Payment to Sgt. Mountford.

Such competitions were regular and popular affairs, with many members of the public coming along to watch. A common and very important prize was a new regulation carbine, perfect for the aspiring marksman. Eventually, firing artillery became possible and the rules were formalized by the National Artillery Association. The NAA was formed at Shoeburyness in 1865 for the purpose of running national competitions and, having visited as spectators in 1868, the 4th Durhams entered their first competition in 1870 where they came third. They felt cheated of the cup and vented their spleen on the umpire, a naturalized German, in song (Hartlepools Association with the Royal Regiment of Artillery, John o'Heugh (John Davidson), author's collection):

> The German Cuss, that ordered things, and placed us at the gun,
> Awarded the 3rd. Northumberland the prize that we had won.
> Oh wasn't that a dirty trick To treat the Durham's so.
> In the days we went to Shoeburyness A short time ago.

All the region's corps continued entering the competitions, with considerable success:

> At the NAA meeting this year the corps had the good fortune to win the Queens Prize for the highest aggregate in the 64 and 40-Pdrs competition, the detachment gaining the 10 Queens Prize Cups (one large for the No. 1 and nine smaller cups for the men, value £100). The home coming of the detachment was made a public reception. They were received at the railway station by a Guard of Honour, under the Command of Captain Middleton, and the station was decorated. The Sheriff and Members of the Corporation met the detachment at the reception room in the station, with many distinguished persons. The health of Lieut. Read, who commanded the Hull detachment at Shoeburyness, was proposed, and also that of the detachment, and speeches were made from the hotel balcony to the parade and public. The procession to the Corps Headquarters was one of enthusiasm, the winners riding on 40-Pdr gun carriages. (Ibid.)

The local gunners were becoming proficient in handling a wide range of guns, although there were still complaints of inadequate time spent practising due to the

Hull Volunteers with Armstrong 40pr RBL, having won the Queens Prize at Shoeburyness in 1879

cost. Following success in the NAA competitions five Durham and four Yorkshire men were sent to Canada in 1884 for the most prestigious event of their history.

On this day the detachment of twenty men chosen to represent British Volunteer Artillery (five of whom were from the 4th DVA), with the addition of Captain J. W. Cameron were practicing at Altcar near Liverpool, before sailing for Canada when Sergeant Major C. I. Smyth made a remarkable score of five direct hits upon a barrel target out of five shots with the 64pr, gun. This team won the cup offered by Queen Victoria for competition between England and Canada. They also won several other prizes.

Competitions remained popular until disbandment of the coast defence forces, and the results were eagerly reported in the local newspapers. Nevertheless, by the turn of the century there was concern that the competitions did not reflect the conditions the gunners would have to work under in action. Attempts were made to introduce a little reality and for the first time sponsorship was made available for competitions on local batteries. One of the first town corporations to donate was West Hartlepool who in 1900 gave 1,000 guineas for a prize cup. This was to be competed for annually on the modern 4.7-in and 6-in guns at the South Gare and Cemetery Batteries.

As the Volunteers' ability to handle artillery improved over the years so did the proficiency of their officers and NCOs. Periodically they were expected to attend various courses but it was not until 1871 that it became compulsory for them to attend the School of Instruction at the Royal Military Repository, where they learnt to dismount, move and remount heavy guns. By 1892 they were expected to have passed the Artillery Certificate and many booklets and articles on the theories of

Hull Volunteer Corps Challenge Cups in 1907 for (left to right) Artillery Shooting, Garrison Competition, Repository, Highest Aggregate and Rangefinding.

coast defence began to circulate. Surprisingly, there was no test of fitness until 1896, when medical examinations became mandatory for new recruits.

As an 'unofficial' force, the Volunteers were never embodied for service overseas, although they offered their services many times. Although members of some engineer and infantry corps did serve in the Boer War, there are no records of local artillerymen serving overseas.

Before leaving the Volunteers it is worth remembering that they were operating deadly weapons and, regardless of their ability, unfortunate accidents were not unknown. The following extracts are from the diaries of Hull RGA:

> In 1872 a lad in Lincolnshire who had found a shell, which no doubt had been fired by the Corps from Paull, was playing with it , when it exploded and injured him. He unfortunately, died from lockjaw through this accident.

> In May 1889, Boatman Strawson, while boating near Marfleet was struck in the thigh by a supposed ricochet bullet while the Corps was at carbine practice and died the same day. The Corps was represented at the funeral and paid all the expenses.

> At gun practice this year (1892) at Paull, through an error, the Range Party was laid on, which resulted in Gunner Cooper being wounded, but, fortunately he was not permanently injured.

> On the 6th August, 1895, James Leggott, a Waterman (and Gunner in the Corps) was killed at the Alexandra Dock by the explosion of a 40pr RBL shell, which had been found near Paull, and given over to Leggott to be sunk in deep water. Instead however, he had brought it to the dock, and was tampering with it.

Hull Volunteer Artillery staff sergeants posing for a formal photograph in 1906.

ROYAL GARRISON ARTILLERY

With the Territorial and Reserve Forces Act of 1907 the Militia and Volunteers ceased to exist. The Volunteers transferred to the Territorial Force and were integrated into the Royal Garrison Artillery and allocated to the coast defences. When war broke out in 1914 these weekend soldiers found themselves having to transform into full-time professionals. Patience, good humour, deep pockets and the occasional blind eye became useful attributes for a senior officer. Lieutenant Colonel Robson, commander of the Hartlepool defences, found himself having to cover for the indiscretion of his men on a number of occasions. One time he was called on by a plain clothes detective demanding the names of men who had stolen from a nearby railway. He could not hide the culprits, as rails were clearly visible, sticking up out of their dugouts, but he did manage to convince the policeman that they were not actually stolen, merely commandeered.

Another incident that made him 'livid' was during live fire practice from the Heugh Battery when a plane flew over, bombed and sank the gunners' target. Robson was struck by the pilot's audacity when on landing he claimed to have engaged and sunk an enemy submarine. Many years later, Robson was able to look back at these incidents and publicly joke about them, but other difficulties must have been more frustrating. After the Bombardment he decided to mount two mobile 4.7-in guns and a searchlight north of the town. The guns could not be acquired through the normal channels but were 'borrowed' from another regiment. Robson paid for the searchlight out of his own pocket and had it delivered to the battery site. The Royal Engineers then buried a cable and covertly tapped into the town's electricity supply. In his own words: 'We couldn't get a brass hat, so we had to do the best we could and I always considered that we were the Cinderella of the coast defences' (*Northern Daily Mail*, 11 Feb. 1932, Durham Heavy Brigade Scrapbook, DCRO, D/DLI6/1/6-7).

The most important post-war events for the gunners were the summer and weekend camps, held at their own batteries or further afield. There was obviously some worry about what the men got up to when away from home. Much effort was made to reassure those left behind that all was well, no mischief was going on and, most importantly, the men were well fed.

The Terriers rise at 6am and parade at 6-30 for physical training. Then there are buttons to be polished (polishing is done every morning and evening), bedding to be put up, and kits to be laid out uniform style. And by the time these little jobs have been completed, one feels ready for breakfast after which the real work of the day begins.

And by the way, regarding our food, mothers need not worry about their sons, or wives about their husbands, whilst sweethearts can dismiss their boyfriends from their minds. Were all being well fed, and Army life seems to be agreeing with everybody. The fellow who mixes in with the 'mob' just can't go wrong. This is a sample of the menu provided for the men: Breakfast - egg and bacon, tea, bread and butter; dinner- meat and the usual vegetables; followed by custard and prunes; tea - sausage and pickles and bread and tea.

All told it's a great life. It's certainly a healthy life, and guaranteed to cure anyone of anything that ails them. In addition the men here have the satisfaction of knowing they're doing their bit in a critical time. (*Northern Daily Mail*, 9 Aug. 1939, Durham Heavy Brigade Scrapbook, DCRO, D/DLI6/1/6-7)

The 'real work of the day' began at 7.00 am with the first parade and inspection by the orderly officer and sergeant, followed by gun crews cleaning their weapons and ready use lockers for further inspection. Lookouts were posted and relieved every hour. While the battery was cleaned up, other men trained on dummy loaders and small arms. They also received physical training and football was a very popular pastime.

Competition remained an important means of training the gunners. Perhaps the most hotly contested in the region was the Northern Command Ladies Cup as it pitted the men from the three defended ports against each other. Points were awarded for various aspects of the men's performance, as can be seen in the table from the results for 1935, won by Tynemouth.

Durham gunners at breech of 9.2-in Mk X

TABLE OF POINTS AWARDED IN THE NORTHERN COMMAND LADIES CUP, 1935

	Possible	Tynemouth	Durham	E. Riding
Clothing/equipment in store	50	43	42	40
Interior economy	75	68	63	69
Fire discipline	100	73	72	55
Gun drill	75	54	67	48
Steadiness and smartness on parade	50	45	40	50
Attendance at camp	100	93	91	65
Total	450	376	375	327

Due to the various economy measures of the 1930s, the competition did not take place every year, but the overall scores were Durham three, Tynemouth two and East Riding one win.

Another important competition was the Kings Prize, which from 1930 included the 9.2-in gun and was competed for by regiments across the country. It comprised twelve rounds fired out to ranges of 8,000 yards, with points awarded for accuracy and rate of fire, a good score being eight hits. Winning a round gave the gunners the chance to go through to another battery which under normal circumstances they would not have visited, such as the Isle of Wight and Penlee at Plymouth. The Durhams' performance was generally good, although they seem to have been plagued with minor mishaps, such as dropping shells and even the electrical leads becoming detached, mirroring events at the Lighthouse gun during the Bombardment.

No competition could truly reflect the conditions that the gunners would be expected to fight under and a number of exercises were carried out during the summer camps to test both men and equipment. Few went completely according to plan, being hampered by ammunition and other shortages. The gunners also had the vagaries of the North-East coast to contend with:

'There had been consistently bad weather during the summer preceding camp but fortunately good conditions prevailed throughout the period with the exception of fog seawards. This together with the fleet of herring drifters coming and going to North Shields, interfered rather with the shooting programme. Three series of 6-in had to be abandoned but the remainder of the programme was successfully carried out.' (North Eastern Gazette, 8 Aug. 1934, Durham Heavy Brigade Scrapbook, DCRO, D/DLI6/1/6-7)

As it was not possible to close a port during peacetime, live firing had to be carried out amidst all the usual maritime comings and goings. On one occasion a fully loaded gun was accidently laid on and almost fired at a passing fishing boat. Such an event was potentially lethal. If communication broke down between the rangefinder and gun, the gunners would not necessarily be aware a mistake had been made.

Occasionally, large-scale exercises took place involving the Navy, although air attack was never simulated, perhaps a tacit recognition that a handful of Lewis guns were never going to provide sufficient protection.

'War was declared by Northland and Southland today, and full preparations are being made by the batteries at the mouth of the Tees to resist an attack by Northland warships and submarines which is expected tomorrow.' The Whisky War came about as a result of friction between Northland and Southland over the production of whisky, an important ingredient of Southland's explosives. The Northland Government had arrested an English scientific mission purportedly searching for the Loch Ness monster, on the grounds of espionage. War was declared. Such was the background story for a two-day exercise in 1934 to test the Tees defences and the new fortress plotting system. The Navy supplied two submarines and two sloops which were to attack the port. The new fortress command post at Todd Point, Warrenby, coordinated the Heugh, Lighthouse, Pasley and South Gare batteries in the examination and counter-bombardment roles against the 'hostile' vessels. Improvisation was to be key: the South Gare Battery had been disarmed in 1920 and was little more than an empty shell. An 18pr field gun was brought into simulate an active battery and field equipment set up to provide communications. Detachments from all three ports were involved; the Durham Heavy Brigade (TA), North Riding Fortress Engineers (TA) and Tyne Electrical Engineers (TA). The exercise was observed by the Commander in Chief of Northern Command, General Sir Alexander Wardrop and Admiral Sir Hugh Tweedie.

The visit of the Elbe in 1936.

The attack commenced at 8.00 am, with the laying of smoke screens, the guns firing blanks and numerous flashes from the engineers' signal lamps. Observers found the atmosphere 'very warlike', though the illusion was spoilt slightly by anglers on the ends of the breakwaters and holiday makers wandering among the 'Tommies'. The examination of the 'enemy' cruisers, HMS *Scout* and *Scimitar*, was undertaken by the steam tug *Lingdale*, which then ordered the shore batteries to open fire. For the many locals who came out to watch, the most exciting spectacles were the night battles when the searchlights were brought into play, sweeping across the bay. No attempt was made to draw too many conclusions from the exercise but it was seen that the coast gunners were equally efficient on their own fixed defences and on hastily deployed field equipment (*Northern Echo*, 9 Aug. 1934, Durham Heavy Brigade Scrapbook, DCRO, D/DLI6/1/6-7).

The following year the gunners were actually to meet the 'enemy' when the German Fisheries gunboat *Elbe* paid a visit to Tynemouth. Friendly relations were cemented during a second visit a year later at Hartlepool when the captain was entertained ashore and Captain Nicholson of Durham Heavy Brigade visited the vessel. It does not seem that the German officers were allowed to visit the gun batteries.

THE SECOND WORLD WAR: A GUNNER REMEMBERS

With the Second World War we enter a period that remains in living memory. Bombardier Len Stockill joined up in 1937, having lied about his age (he was 16), and served at the Heugh Battery.

He joined just after the Heugh and Lighthouse Battery had been amalgamated: Heugh No. 1 gun had been removed, leaving two 6-in Mk VII, one at each site. He was called up for two weeks in 1938 during the Munich Crisis and then permanently on 23 August 1939 at the outbreak of the Second World War. The batteries can fairly be described as run down and much work was needed to bring them up to standard. Having stood more or less empty for twenty years the most pressing problem was housing and looking after the men, not only the gunners but others also stationed on the Headland. Commandeering local houses helped ease the situation:

Bdr L. Stockill in full dress uniform.

> We had all the houses in Moor Terrace up to and including the Rovers Club and also the last two in Cliff Terrace. The end one was used as a medical centre and the other one was the officers quarters and mess. These premises were taken over very quickly due to poor accommodation within the battery. As you can imagine the amenities were not good for two hundred plus men and officers.

We rigged up a temporary cookhouse and to help there was also an old fashioned field kitchen on wheels used mainly for hot water. This was manned by Gunner Stump. Now for 'Stumpy' to mash the tea, someone had to tip the dry tea into the water whilst Stump stood by with a ladle of water to put the fire out so the tea did not boil, you can imagine the clouds of steam coming back from the fire, poor old 'Stumpy' was as black as a fire back. (Stockill letters.)

Even in their commandeered accommodation the men suffered hardships, particularly in keeping clean and warm, as this was dependent on a limited coal supply.

There were many men to a room and nearly all the rooms had fireplaces, so there was a coal ration. Now in the cold weather we had to go easy, but not all did. The coal store was in the corner of the Lighthouse Battery yard with an eight foot wall around it plus a gate. Now one man, who I won't name, climbed over the wall and started to throw lumps of coal over the wall to be picked up and put in his bucket. Whilst this was going on Major Eddowes, (the Assistant Fire Commander) was making a walk round and after dodging pieces of coal waited till the man climbed back over into his arms. He let him keep the coal but the next morning he was put on a charge and had to appear before the said Major. The punishment he got was fourteen days confined to barracks plus two separate hours of pack drill on the promenade.

The accommodation and battery facilities were greatly improved in the summer of 1940 when strenuous efforts were made to secure the coastline. With so much land now temporarily in military hands it was possible to extend the battery sites and start building outside the original boundaries. The Town Moor behind the Heugh Battery became home to a new cookhouse, numerous huts and a battery plotting room. One lieutenant began to consider the ground defences for the battery. His answer, much derided by the gunners, was to dig a long trench complete with fire bays and barbed wire entanglements. The work was duly carried out and soon nicknamed 'Brockhurst's Folly' after its instigator. It was never manned but did present an effective obstacle to men returning from an illicit night on the town. Len found himself on one occasion having to recover a drunken comrade who had fallen asleep on the wire one frosty night.

A young gunner from 187 Bty Durham Heavy Brigade.

Although the guns were never fired in anger during the Second World War, there were occasional opportunities for the gunners to get to grips with unwary vessels and enemy aircraft.

A couple of times we put a shot across the bows of a ship that slipped by the Examination Vessel that was moored in the bay. The shell was not explosive, it was flat ended which when fired made a lot of noise and a big splash. One day a Dornier aeroplane was machine gunning the Examination Vessel and our Lewis gun opened up on it. We heard that it crashed inland and was riddled with bullet holes. I'm told the Lewis gunner got off two magazines.

Most days were not so eventful and Len gives us a good idea of a normal day which is applicable not only throughout the region but also very similar to those of the First World War.

First parade was at seven o'clock (revallie at 6 o'clock). This was for roll call and inspection by the Orderly Officer and Sergeant. The gun crews on duty (24hrs) went their respective guns for cleaning and general inspection of the shell and cartridge ready use lockers. When all this was done a 'lookout' was posted with a relief every hour. Other crews not on duty did various jobs round the battery such as general cleaning, 24 hour guard duty, leave (local) also drills such as on the dummy loader, marching, small arms training and not forgetting Physical Training. The guard duty was for 24 hrs, 16:00 to 16:00 the next day. The guard consisted of five men with an NCO, in charge and they would be fell in on the parade ground. The inspection was very keen and the best turned out man was given stick guard. This meant he didn't do any sentry duty day or night, he also had to fetch tea in the early morning and relieve the sentries for meals.

There was fierce competition to be the smartest and we even burnished the correct number of studs on our boots and polished the soles. I remember one instance when some of my pals carried me by my elbows from my hut to the parade ground so I didn't get the soles dirty. Another trick was when you cleaned your rifle, for the last pull through you used a wad of silver paper which imparted a good shine to the bore.

Each the day duty officer and sergeant were put on the notice board along with duty gun crews, and names of 24 hour guard. Other information went on such as courses and War Office instructions. It was the Battery Sergeant Major, the senior NCO, along with sergeants, bombardiers and lance bombardiers who carried out the day to day running of the battery.

Ships are well known for their cats but it seems that the gunners' favourite was the dog. The 'old battery dog' barked at the raiders during the Bombardment and a photograph taken that day shows four dogs, one at the gunners' feet and the others cradled in their arms. Later, in the Second World War:

Training on the dummy loader at Heugh Battery.

Dogs always seem to have been around, we had four and they always hung around a certain gunner, two of them were really mangy. One day they were fighting outside the guardroom where I was guard NCO. Anyway I grabbed these two and got bitten in the process much to the anger of the orderly officer who told another gunner to get rid of them. Now this other gunner, the dog man aforementioned, had also got a very small terrier which followed him all over, even on gun watch. One of his tricks was to open the breech, pop the little dog in the barrel then run to the muzzle for the dog to jump out.

When the batteries went into care and maintenance between 1943 and 1944 the gunners were distributed into other services. Bdr Stockill was soon to find himself in far more inhospitable circumstances, serving on the Arctic convoys.

I joined the navy because of the War Office instructions requesting volunteers. Prior to this I had volunteered for the glider pilots, airborne and others but the Battery Commander would not let me go then as I was too useful as an instructor.

When the batteries were reactivated in 1947 it did not go down well in all quarters. In fact, by 1954 strong opposition led to a flurry of letters in the local press. This extract, from a disgruntled Whitley Bay resident, appeared in the Newcastle Journal.

A great number consider the selection of a densely populated residential area for practice by day and night with fairly massive artillery to have been a piece of arrant stupidity which only the military mind could have conceived.

We object very strongly indeed to this intolerable racket which has been inflicted without the slightest consideration for the civilian population.

We know that pat will come the answer 'Ah but training is necessary at

Len Stockill discussing the restoration of the Heugh Battery in 2003 with John Southcott of the Heugh Gun Battery Trust.

the point from which the guns will fire in time of war. You who grumble now will change your tune when an enemy fleet sails up the Tyne. You are being unpatriotic in resenting these fine bangs.

Even conceding the possible usefulness of these guns, modern plotting methods and the use of radar make nonsense of this argument. A range on some remote stretch of uninhabited coast would serve exactly the same purpose as Tynemouth Castle and the Army need not pretend otherwise.

What would be lacking and herein might lie the real reason for Tynemouth having been chosen are hotels, pubs, cinemas and other amenities.

Evidently it was not only the noise of the guns that angered the residents but also the incidents of drunken horseplay that went with the summer camps. Even the officers were not above enjoying themselves, as recorded by Major Nixon in his digest:

An enjoyable, though somewhat riotous Guest Night was held on Wednesday, 5th August when the Regimental Band excelled itself, particularly by misunderstanding the Adjutants signal for silence when grace was about to be said, and giving instead a thunderous rendering of the National Anthem. After a very good meal the party descended on the Mess Marquee, which was unfortunately wrecked before the departure of the Brigade Commander. A sail maker was busily employed the following day making a new one. It is on record that the Adjutant failed to climb through the marquee vent, and that Major Nixon could not be induced to make the attempt (even though I say it myself). (Digest of Regimental Activities, 1953, Durham Heavy Brigade Scrapbook, DCRO, D/DLI6/1/6-7)

THE BOMBARDMENT OF HARTLEPOOL

And so it came about that on a bright, sunny morning in December, when a lifting haze covered the sea, as it does sometimes in mellow autumn, when the wavelets just turned over on the limestone beach like the soft petals of chrysanthemums, when half the world was only half awake, when the children were getting into their stride for school and the workman was looking for his breakfast - then the German vomit was thrown on battery, beach, and the thickly peopled streets of the two Hartlepools, to defile, desecrate and destroy. *(Frederick Miller*, Under Shell Fire: The Hartlepools Scarborough and Whitby under German Shell Fire' *(Robert Martin Ltd, 1915))*

The German naval raid at Hartlepool on Wednesday, 16 December 1914, was the only time that Britain's coast defences were involved in protecting the country from a hostile sea-borne force. Later, the Second World War would see cross-channel duels between British and German batteries and attempts to sink shipping in the English Channel, while other guns opened fire on and in some cases sank friendly vessels but the 'Bombardment' of Hartlepool was Britain's only classic

Sketch by James Clarke showing where the first shells fell, with the Lighthouse Battery in the background.

engagement between battleship and battery. The event carries other historical undertones as it was here that the first military and civilian casualties of the First World War fell on home soil and it was also for this action that the first Military Medals to be struck were awarded. The same day saw attack on Scarborough and Whitby but the story of those places is not covered here as neither was armed and events in all three towns, as seen from a civilian perspective, have been well documented by other authors.

At the outbreak of the First World War the Committee of Imperial Defence concluded that the greatest threat posed by the German High Seas Fleet was to enable an invasion of up to 70,000 men before the Royal Navy could intervene. They also feared full-scale naval confrontation as, although they might win a decisive battle, their forces risked being be severely depleted. Each threat raised distinct problems, countering an invasion required a rapid response, which effectively meant dispersing the fleet along the coast, while fighting a major sea battle called for a concentration of forces. Naval policy held the bulk of the fleet at Scapa Flow in Orkney, ostensibly out of reach of enemy submarines and from where it was believed a decisive hammer blow could be struck should the High Seas Fleet venture from their home ports. This effectively contained the High Seas Fleet in the North Sea but no attempt was made to blockade their home ports as this might lead to an unplanned large-scale engagement. Rather the Navy tried to assert their authority with a policy of sweeping the North Sea, to which the Germans usually responded with a rapid retreat. The first engagement took place at Heligoland Bight on 28 August 1914, when three German light cruisers were sunk. These losses caused an already cautious High Seas Fleet to become even more circumspect and the Kaiser personally to insist that large-scale battles were to be avoided, believing that an intact fleet would be a very powerful bargaining tool in future negotiations. Nevertheless, some form of action was necessary for morale as the fleet could not be seen to be idle in port while the brunt of war fell on the troops on the Western Front. Admiral von Ingenohl, Commander in Chief of the German Fleet, proposed a policy of *Kleinkrieg* (little war) to comprise U-boat attack, mine laying, coastal raiding and bombardment.

The first attack came on 3 November 1914 at Great Yarmouth but comprised little more than a futile long-range shelling of the beach, coupled with mine laying. A fisheries protection gunboat, the *Halcyon*, equipped with only two 4.7-in and four 6pr guns, attempted to intervene but was hit eight times before being rescued by a destroyer laying down a protective smokescreen. A pursuit by submarines was attempted but unfortunately they found themselves among British mines and submarine *D5* was lost, with twenty of her crew. SMS *Yorck*, one of the raiders, then fell to German mines as she lost her course in fog while entering the Jade. Although the raid was ineffective, it served to bring invasion fears to the fore, as the Germans had been seen to strike without warning or reprisal.

The Committee of Imperial Defence had estimated that Britain would need 300,000 soldiers to resist an invasion, but few were available as all resources were being sent to stabilize the Western Front and the Naval Commander in Chief, Admiral Sir John Jellicoe, came under great pressure to disperse his fleet to protect the coast. A partial compromise was reached and the fleet split, so that twenty-three battleships remained at Scapa Flow, nine were sent to bolster the old fleet of pre-dreadnoughts at Sheerness, while a further nine were split between Rosyth, Tyne and Humber. First Sea Lord Admiral Sir John 'Jackie' Fisher felt that Jellicoe's redistribution was insufficient and, predicting further attacks, wrote to him on 28 November:

> You won't have a look in if the German battle cruisers come out, as they will hustle over and hustle back after bombarding, but I hope we will catch them with our submarines and our destroyers, but I see no way of preventing their coming to bombard, as we have nothing south to meet them. What a howl there will be! (J M Ward, Dawn Raid: The Bombardment of the Hartlepools *(Printability Publishing, 1989), p. 2)*

Buoyed by the inability of the Royal Navy to frustrate the Great Yarmouth raid, Ingenohl planned a far more ambitious attack. He had a number of objectives. Primarily, it was hoped that pursuing British battleships would be lured into mines, some of which were to be laid during the raid, and then drawn into an engagement where they were at a serious disadvantage. It was also intended to bring the war home to the British public and, by proving that the Navy offered no protection, increase calls for troops to be kept in the country for coast defence. The targets, Hartlepool, Scarborough and Whitby, were well chosen as this part of the East coast was remote from both Scapa Flow and Sheerness, and the raid could be carried out before the Navy, as a whole, had time to intervene. Contrary to popular opinion, naval bombardment of centres of population was a justifiable tactic of war as the relevant article of the Hague Convention had not actually been ratified. British propaganda made much of the fact that Scarborough and Whitby were undefended towns but grudgingly had to admit that the attack on Hartlepool, where the bulk of the casualties occurred, was in fact legitimate. Admiral Fisher received early warning of the attack from naval intelligence at Room 40 who, following the capture of a number of German codebooks, were now becoming adept at predicting German intentions. Although the date was reasonably definite, the location was unclear and, as only one squadron was anticipated to attack, only a small force was prepared to intercept. Originally the date chosen for the attack was 29 November 1914 and a submarine, *U-27*, commanded by Captain Lieutenant Wegener was sent out to reconnoitre the coast around Whitby, in particular to investigate for minefields. Nothing suspicious was noted and the free movement of merchant shipping off the coast suggested that the area was free of mines and the circumstances for an attack good. Deteriorating weather intervened and worrying reports of heavy gunfire off the coast at Hartlepool on the night of 23 November, indicating the presence of a large British force, led to the attack being postponed. *U-27* was sent out to reconnoitre once again on the 28 November, followed by *U-28* and *U-32* which took up post off the Humber to obstruct any intervention by the Navy from that direction during the raid.

On the 13 December *U-27* returned to Dogger Bank where Captain Lieutenant Wegener signalled that conditions were good for the attack. Admiral Hipper, who

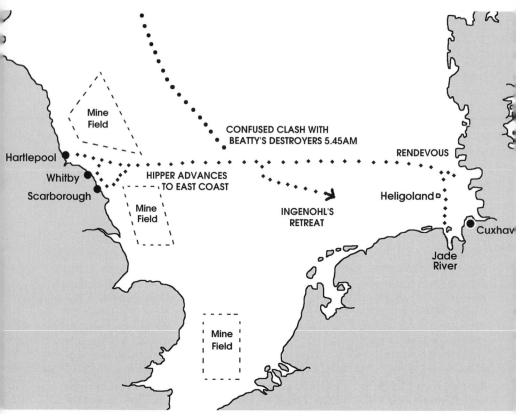

North Sea naval movements leading to the Bombardment.

would lead the raid, ordered it to take place on 16 December. On the 15th he boarded SMS *Seydlitz* to lead the First Scouting Group comprising the battlecruisers *Moltke*, *Von der Tann*, *Derfflinger* and the older armoured cruiser Blucher out from the Jade to rendezvous with Admiral von Ingenohl north of Heligoland. Ingenohl's force comprised fourteen dreadnoughts, eight pre-dreadnoughts, two armoured cruisers, six light cruisers and fifty destroyers, while a third squadron were also making their way to the rendezvous point, where all would wait until the hours of darkness before continuing with their mission. It was hoped to lure approximately ten British battleships out into the North Sea where they could be overwhelmed. Under the cover of darkness, Hipper then left the group, taking his squadron off to the North-East coast.

Room 40 had been monitoring the German wireless traffic but had only identified Ingenohl's force and the Admiralty, unaware that the majority of the High Seas Fleet were at sea, sent a small group under Admiral Sir David Beatty to intercept. Hampered by worsening seas and mists the two forces met in darkness in the early hours of the 16th and a confused long-range exchange of fire took

SMS Seydlitz

place. Ingenohl, believing he was facing the full force of the British Navy and unaware of his own superiority, retreated and returned to base as per the Kaiser's orders. This was a potentially catastrophic course of action, as it would leave Hipper to return unsupported having expended much of his ammunition on bombarding two seaside towns and a minor commercial port.

Heavy seas forced Hipper to send his three light cruisers and destroyers home and now he faced a difficult decision. His return was unprotected and lacking the shield of his destroyers he was dependent on speed, rough seas and fog for his safe return. Fog was a major concern: it might well protect him but it could also shroud his targets, forcing him very close to the shore even just to find out where he was. He also had good reason to give up as Ingenohl by retiring had aborted the main objective as the High Seas Fleet was no longer in position for the anticipated ambush. Hipper took the gamble and pressed on, passing through the gap in the minefields east of Whitby before sending the vessels to their targets: *Kolberg* to lay mines off Filey, *Von der Tann* and *Derfflinger* to bombard Scarborough and Whitby, while he led *Seydlitz, Moltke* and *Blucher* toward Hartlepool. As they approached the coast, Ober Leuitnant Ahlefeld, who had spent the previous weeks aboard U-27 and knew the East coast the best, took over navigation on the *Seydlitz*.

Two of the battlecruisers that attacked Hartlepool were of the latest type. *Seydlitz* and *Moltke* were each well armed, with a main armourment of ten 28 cm (11-in) guns supplemented with twelve 15 cm (5.9-in) guns and four 15 cm torpedo tubes. They differed mainly in that *Seydlitz*, the newer ship, was protected with heavier armour and was consequently slightly slower, with a speed of 26.5 knots compared to 28 knots. The third ship, the *Blucher* was older and smaller, armed with twelve 21 cm (8.2-in) guns and eight 15 cm guns. She was also the slowest, with a top speed of 25 knots.

Blucher was to engage the batteries at Hartlepool and broadsides from her 8.2-

SMS Moltke

Lt Colonel Robson, the fortress commander.

in, while perhaps not destroying them, should certainly keep the gunners sufficiently distracted to allow *Seydlitz* and *Moltke* to bring their larger guns to bear on the town unmolested. Just to make sure, the larger vessels would spend the first few minutes of the fire-fight pumping 11-in shells into the emplacements.

In December 1914 Hartlepool was defended by three 6-in guns at the Heugh and Lighthouse Batteries, while to the south the Tees was protected by two 4.7-in guns at South Gare Battery. A third 4.7-in gun was being mounted on the Old Pier to serve as the examination battery and its searchlight, the only one at that time in Hartlepool, was already working. Lieutenant Colonel Lancelot Robson, the local fire commander, had proposed extra guns to the north of the town but work was yet to start. Robson had in fact retired three days after the outbreak of war in August but had promptly been recalled the same day by telephone to take temporary control of the Tees and Hartlepool defences, only to be replaced two weeks later and given the joint positions of fire commander and second in command of the Durham RGA. This was an enviable and powerful position as the usual friction between the two commands no longer applied and he could ensure his orders were promptly carried out. There was, as he put it, 'no back chat'.

He was well qualified: at 59 years of age he had served on the Hartlepool guns for forty years, been a keen member of the RML competition crews and gained his commission in 1890. He had long petitioned for changes in the town's defences, perhaps the most significant being a wooden screen placed at the back of the Heugh Battery, which caused it to appear higher than it was.

With his new-found authority he made two important changes. In November he moved his own command post from the Fairy Cove rangefinder into the Heugh Battery command post or 'lookout' as a temporary measure until a purpose-built tower in the battery was ready. Secondly, in October he had succeeded in moving the coastguard from their hut on the Town Moor into the lighthouse as a makeshift port war signal station, pending their move into the same tower. The original posts had been set up during the final years of the old Cemetery Battery and now that it was closed they were too far north and 'strung out' to serve the remaining guns effectively. The works had been supplemented by a number of trenches and 'splinter proofs' along the coast - built by men on their way to the Western Front.

The mobilization of the Durham Royal Garrison Artillery, who manned the guns, had gone reasonably well. The gunners were on their way to summer camp at Broughty Ferry when the order came through and they were promptly turned around at Newcastle railway station. Among the usual difficulties of installing men in their new billets and banning them from the local entertainments, the only incident of note had been the accidental shooting of a Gunner Mews in the ankle by Gunner Lee while on guard duty at the port war signal station. Fortunately,

The layout of the Hartlepool defences, 1914

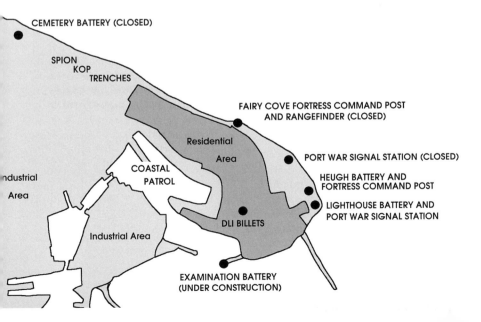

CEMETERY BATTERY (CLOSED)

SPION KOP TRENCHES

FAIRY COVE FORTRESS COMMAND POST AND RANGEFINDER (CLOSED)

Residential Area

PORT WAR SIGNAL STATION (CLOSED)

Industrial Area

COASTAL PATROL

HEUGH BATTERY AND FORTRESS COMMAND POST

LIGHTHOUSE BATTERY AND PORT WAR SIGNAL STATION

DLI BILLETS

Industrial Area

EXAMINATION BATTERY (UNDER CONSTRUCTION)

Gunner Mews recovered quickly and both men went on to serve during the Bombardment.

A number of infantry units were billeted in the town and outlying villages. The 18th Battalion Durham Light Infantry (PALS) were assigned to close defence of the batteries and beach north of the town, under the command of Major Trisram, while trenches at Seaton were manned by a company of the 3rd Yorkshires under Captain Rolls.

The shore defences were supplemented by a coastal patrol, comprising two light cruisers, four destroyers and a submarine, stationed in the harbour. The light cruisers HMS *Patrol* and *Forward* were each armed with nine 4-in guns and two torpedo tubes and had a top speed of 25 knots. HMS *Doon*, *Moy* and *Waveney*, dating from 1903-4, were River 'E' Class destroyers, carrying four 12pr guns and two 18.5 inch torpedo tubes and capable of a relatively fast 25.5 knots. HMS *Test* was classified as an 'E' Class destroyer for convenience, having been launched slightly later in 1909 but with an almost identical specification to the others. Rounding off the coast patrol was submarine *C9*. Armed with two 18-in torpedo tubes she had a top speed of only 13.5 knots and, in common with all submarines of her class, had to be brought to the surface to fire. The potential of submarines to deter opportunistic raiding was recognized by their dispersal. None were located further north than Blyth, where six were placed to defend the Tyne while twenty-one were placed at Harwich, with three allotted to the ports of Hartlepool, Humber and Yarmouth.

At the same time that Beatty's battlecruisers had been sent to intercept Ingenohl's force, the Admiralty sent a series of telegrams to the fortress commanders along the East coast. One arrived at Hartlepool at about midnight of the 15th.

A special sharp lookout to be kept along all East Coast at dawn tomorrow December 16th. Keep fact of special warning as secret as possible; only responsible officers making arrangements to know. - Troopers, London.

It was read by Colonel Hammond, commanding officer, Tees and Hartlepool Defences, and sent on to Lieutenant Colonel Robson, headquartered in the Grand Hotel, West Hartlepool, who added a footnote.

In connection with above the Fortress Commander wishes you to take post from 7.00-8.30 am. If all quiet at latter hour troops may return to billets.

A warning was also sent to the Admiral of Patrols, Commodore First Class, George Ballard ordering the coastal patrol to sea. Taking account of worsening sea conditions, he ordered that the dawn sweeps should continue as normal but other vessels should stay in port, building up steam and ready to go in case a raid developed. At Hartlepool the four destroyers, HMS *Test*, *Moy*, *Doon* and *Waveney* left their anchorage at 5.45 am to commence their usual patrol up and down the coast. Remaining at berth, making ready were the light cruisers HMS *Patrol* and *Forward* alongside submarine *C9*.

Further warnings also seem to have been issued and a 15-year-old telephone attendant at North Eastern Railways received a call from the district intelligence officer requesting that lights be dimmed and the telephone not be used under any circumstances.

Lieutenant Colonel Robson saw no need to make any special preparations apart from his own early attendance at the batteries, for which he booked a car. He was satisfied that the batteries and men were well prepared and his standing orders meant the guns would be manned an hour before daybreak. On his arrival he conferred with his battery commanders and, given the vagueness of the order, they decided that there was no need to warn and perhaps alarm the men but agreed, should nothing transpire, they would give the men the afternoon off. Lieutenant Colonel Robson quietly went up into the battery command post at the Heugh Battery, leaving the rest of the arrangements to the battery commanders, brothers Captain Oscar Trenchmann at the Heugh Battery and Lieutenant Richard ('Dickie') Trenchmann at the Lighthouse Battery.

Captain Oscar Trenchmann, the Heugh Battery commander.

As a precaution, Captain Oscar Trenchmann made some changes to the men who would man the guns and a number of district gunners were assigned, which pleased the master gunner as for a day at least he was freed from the drudgery of ledgers and paperwork. The men in the magazines were also regulars and, although the bulk of the crew, Territorials, formed a tightly knit group, there was no resentment at the changes. The calibrations and testing of guns and rangefinder went smoothly and by 6.30 am Bombardiers Mallin and Hope, the morning's gun captains, reported that the guns were ready.

It was dark and cold when we turned out in the early morning and after partaking of a pot of hot coffee and a biscuit we quietly prepared the guns for action. About half past six a whisper went round that the Colonel was in the Battery, 'There's something up' someone remarked. (Anonymous gunner quoted in *Ward, Dawn Raid, p. 39*)

Shortly after 7.30 am a small contingent of 18th Battalion Durham Light Infantry, singing 'Tipperary', marched the short distance from their billets at the Borough Hall to the batteries. Others on different details took up position at various points around the town. Each had been issued with 250 rounds for their Lee Enfields, but a shortage of webbing meant that bullets were stuffed into greatcoat pockets and bayonets tied to their belts with string. One group came into the Heugh Battery to collect a Maxim gun and tripod from the old magazine, which they set up in a 'beach situated machine gun nest' overlooking the promenade and sea between the batteries. Among them were Private Theo Jones, Private Turner and Lance Corporal Clark, under the command of Corporal Liddle. Nearby, a group of Royal

Engineers casually chatted, having watched the gunners drill.

Once the batteries were prepared, most of the gunners were dismissed to the warmth of the shelters where some managed to doze. Others remained at their posts and Harry Tyson and Jack Wilkinson, having been assigned to lookout duty were ordered to march between the Heugh guns with bayonets fixed.

As dawn rose, the destroyers of the coastal patrol under Lieutenant Commander Fraser turned south to continue their sweep past Teesmouth and at 7.40 am came in closer to shore than usual to clear a bank of fog lying 4,000 yards offshore and exchanged signals with the port war signal station at the Lighthouse Battery before returning back into the mist.

Approaching from the south-east the German battlecruisers broke through the mist at 8.00 am to come within sight of land for the first time. Hipper's gamble had paid off, the coast was clear of fog but it was apparent that they would have to come in close to the shore and would be well within range of the town's defences. The raiders were soon spotted by South Gare PWSS who signalled them and telephoned Lieutenant Colonel. Robson at the Heugh Battery and a brief exchange took place:

PWSS: Three warships coming in at great speed.

Robson: What Class and Nationality?

PWSS: They are our ships, they are flying the White Ensign and have answered our signal. (L Robson, 'Bombardment of Hartlepools', Journal of Royal Artillery, XLVIII (1921))

The German battlecruisers were soon seen by Lieutenant Commander Fraser aboard HMS *Doon*, who was under no doubt of their nationality and immediately ordered an attack. At 9,000 yards they were well out of reach of his destroyer's 12pr

The coast patrol engages the German vessels.

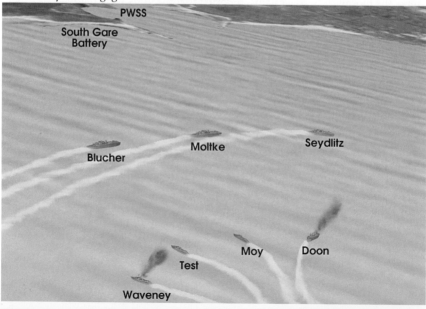

guns, which at any range would hardly have inconvenienced such vessels. He led the destroyers through rolling swell into a hail of fire in an attempt to press home a torpedo attack. The force of fire proved too much for *Waveney, Moy* and *Test* which soon veered off to the north. *Doon* continued, closing the range to 5,000 yards until she was finally forced to break off and began to flounder, having taken a number of hits. James Fraser, a stoker, had been killed and eight other seamen wounded. The other destroyers had escaped with only light damage and fortunately no casualties, with *Waveney* emerging from the encounter unscathed. Admiral Hipper, believing that the *Doon* was sinking and having seen the other destroyers scatter ordered that they be left alone. He had no intention of wasting time that would be better spent bombarding the town. Lieutenant Commander Fraser immediately set about putting his vessel in order and some work was required to repair the aerial for the wireless set, as it took twenty minutes before he could get a signal explaining his predicament to the Admiralty.

A gunner at the Lighthouse Battery had also seen the battlecruisers approach. He felt a surge of pride as they were the most magnificent vessels he had ever seen and surely, he thought, fine examples of the might of the Royal Navy. His pride turned to thrill as their guns painted the early morning sky orange and blazed away at some unseen enemy out at sea. The thunder of the guns caused a wave of excitement to pass through the batteries and many gunners raised their heads, straining to watch this unexpected naval duel passing before their eyes.

Boom! Boom! went their guns but the ships were firing out to sea and not at us. I strained my eyes to see them and, if possible what they were firing at. My comrades were similarly employed and from the gun platforms and top of mounds watched the incoming vessels and speculated as to the nature of the fight going on at sea. I noticed that all the time, our guns which were loaded, were kept *trained on the ships.'*
(*Anonymous gunner quoted in Ward*, Dawn Raid, *p. 40*)

While the encounter was under way Lieutenant Colonel Robson remained on the phone to South Gare. From the battery commander's post his view south was blocked by the lighthouse and, although he could not see them, he was rightly becoming convinced that the approaching ships were German and their target was the coastal patrol. Unfortunately, South Gare had not only mistaken the German flag for the White Ensign but also identified the ships as being of Indomitable class.

Robson: What are they firing at?

PWSS: I presume at the enemy.

Robson: Are you sure they're not firing at our own destroyers?

PWSS: I can't see what they're firing at. (W A Murley, 'The Bombardment of the Hartlepools', *Journal of Royal Artillery*, LXI (1934))

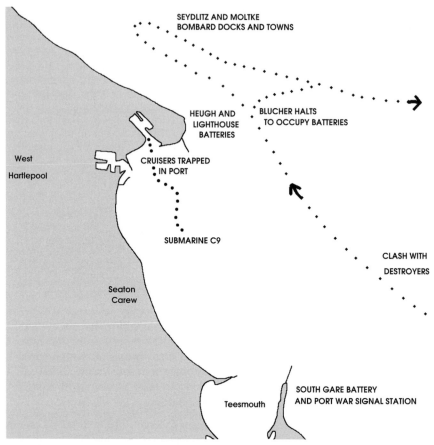

Naval movements on the morning of 16 December 1914.

The battery commander at South Gare was also confused as to the nature of the fight going on out at sea and, by the time the mistake was realized, the battlecruisers, pretty much obscured by mist, had steamed out of range of the battery's two 4.7-in guns unchallenged. The supporting infantry had been ordered to be ready to move anywhere along the coast they might be required but, having assembled, found themselves without cover and had been ordered to lie flat on the breakwater road during the battle.

On hearing the firing Captain Oscar Trenchmann at the Heugh Battery ordered the gun crews out of their shelters and took up position on the parapet above the magazine where he had a clear view of both guns. Gunners Tyson and Wilkinson were ordered off lookout duty on the aprons and to their posts at No. 1 gun as Number 2 and Loading Number. A few last minute changes were made and a long-serving district gunner was also placed on gun No. 1. He turned to the other gunners and grinned broadly: 'Lads, I have been waiting for this for the last eighteen bloody years, let's give 'em the works!' (S. Roberts, lecture on bombardment, 1976).

It was not long before a battleship steamed into view from behind the lighthouse and Captain Oscar Trenchmann quickly ordered both guns to be laid on the vessel. Lieutenant Colonel Robson could not see the reported White Ensign and was perturbed to see the ship was painted the trademark grey of a German battleship. Standing by him, the rangefinder crew were also puzzled: South Gare had stated they were of Indomitable class, but this vessel had two funnels, not three. He tried to stay out of the way of the rangefinder crew as they took their bearings and calmly made their corrections. Looking out of the open door he saw the guns slowly follow the ship in synchronization with the rangefinder. At the Lighthouse Battery Lieutenant 'Dickie' Trenchmann had already ordered the rangefinder and gun to track the last battlecruiser, the *Blucher*, as according to the fire plan the leading pair would be dealt with by the Heugh. The rangefinder pit was out in the open, protected only by a flimsy corrugated iron roof and from his position between it and the gun he could clearly hear the calm, flat voice of the No. 1, Sergeant Major Tom Pailor, as he periodically read out the range.

A slight pause followed at the Heugh, as bemused men watched both the ships and for any signs from their own officers. Again the sky flared orange, this time followed by a huge crash as shells slammed into the houses just behind the lighthouse. To the men it appeared that the Lighthouse Battery was consumed in a cloud of dust and thick white smoke. At a range of 4,150 yards, the *Seydlitz* had fired the first salvo of the Bombardment.

The first shot, I think it was an 11-in shell, carried away the concrete wall on the right corner of the Battery and killed the sentry and 3 other men of the 18th DLI. Another shell which came directly after killed two of our men who had gone to the assistance of the first men who fell. (Anonymous gunner, quoted in Ward, *Dawn Raid*, p. 40)

Then all of a sudden the three ships gave us a broadside. Captain Trenchmann called 'Action', he was the officer who directed fire that morning. (Gunner H Tyson, ibid., p. 62)

At their post by the back wall of the Lighthouse Battery, stretcher bearers Gunners Houston and Spence felt the ground shake as the first shells fell around them. Through the smoke they saw wreckage and wounded men where the machine gun had been and without hesitation ran towards it. Private Theo Jones was evidently dead, while Lance Corporal Clark, Turner and Corporal Liddle were badly wounded if not dying. Looking around they saw that the battery itself was unscathed but the houses behind had taken a severe battering. It was to be their last sight, rounds from a second salvo arrived, sweeping away both wounded and their would-be rescuers.

More men ran to assist, including an officer who found himself temporarily distracted by the behaviour of one of his infantrymen who refused to take cover but persisted in continuing up and down doing his best 'Buckingham Palace' march. The man had been assigned to guard duty and, on seeing his dead and wounded comrades, felt rising panic and feared he would run away. He decided the only thing he could do was obey his orders to the letter and redoubled his efforts.

Lieutenant Colonel Robertson, a doctor in civilian life and the battery medical officer, was at home having breakfast when the gunfire first sounded. He was unaware of the warning and had no reason to be in the battery so early. Knowing that no firing drill was planned he rushed into his uniform, grabbed his bike and made his way to the battery as quickly as possible. It was not easy to get past the townsfolk who now milled around the streets, some were excited by the noise and were racing towards the promenade for a better view while others were intent on getting away as quickly as possible. He finally arrived, having had to spend as much time walking as cycling but any horror the scene before him may have evoked was soon dispelled by an unusual 'comrade': 'The guns were going by that time and the first thing that cheered me was the sight of the old battery dog barking away beside the guns! So then I knew it was alright.' (*Northern Daily Mail*, 29 March 1935).

Using his telephone, Lieutenant Colonel Robson attempted to call the Lighthouse Battery, only to find that the line was dead and, even worse, he could not even talk to his own battery. Peering out into the smoke and dust that almost shrouded the lighthouse he realized that the telephone lines had been brought down by the shells which had fallen near the battery entrance. It must have caused him some anger: for some time he had argued that the 'airlines' were not suitable and that cables should have been routed underground. Unable to issue orders to his battery commanders, he was nevertheless relieved to see all three guns firing of their own accord. The batteries were now acting under standing orders and he resigned himself to the fact that he was only to be an observer to the engagement and not an active participant.

Lieutenant 'Dickie' Trenchmann at the Lighthouse Battery had ordered fire as soon as the first shells hit. The task was not easy, Sergeant Major Tom Pailor, working the rangefinder, could hardly see the target through the smoke.

I will never forget 'Captain' Dickie Trenchmann pacing about calmly and collected as a funeral undertaker, with his monocle exactly in position and staring through it with hardly a trace of perturbation. (Sgt Major T Pailor, quoted in Ward, *Dawn Raid*, p. 48)

Their first high explosive shell fell short and the second also. Firing was painfully slow and so bad was the visibility that the range had to be shortened by 2,000 yards for the third shot. Gun Captain Jack Farmer cheered loudly at his men as they scored a direct hit at 4,000 yards which blew away part of the *Blucher's* forebridge. The shell also disabled two 5.9-in guns and killed nine German seamen. Sergeant Major Tom Pailor felt his initial excitement give way to a cold deliberation and was surprised at the lack of fear he felt. The fourth shell was loaded but misfired, a quick check showed that the 'A' lead carrying the electric charge to fire the cartridge had become detached. Drill dictated that the cartridge should be left in the barrel for ten minutes as a lingering ember could cause it to fire it at any time. Realizing that this would mean that the gun was effectively out of action, Sergeant Douthwaite ordered the men away from the emplacement and, at great risk, withdrew it and placed it in a bucket of water. For this he would later receive the Distinguished Conduct Medal. The fifth shell was fired by percussion, but without cheer: it fell short.

The Heugh Battery engaged the German ships just after the Lighthouse gun fired. Following the fire plan, both guns engaged the same target, the northern-most ship, the *Seydlitz*. Both guns began firing electrically and, as with the Lighthouse gun, both suffered misfires. Gun No. 1 failed first after only two shots and several minutes were lost as the changeover to percussion firing was made. Gun No. 2 performed better and managed to get off thirty rounds before it too failed. Failure of the electric firing meant that the guns had to switch over to the less effective autosights.

Lieutenant Colonel Robson in the lookout was becoming frustrated. Without a working telephone, he was now as isolated as he had ever been in the old post at Fairy Cove. Even worse, the rangefinder crew were finding it almost impossible to get an accurate bearing, due to vibration from the nearby gun. His adjutant Captain Walsh stood beside him as it became clear that their post could easily be smashed at any moment and, although the battery was working well under standing orders, their duty was clear and they decided to remain in the lookout. Picking up a megaphone Robson shouted his decision down to Oscar Trenchmann before returning to his seat. In a moment of quiet contemplation he compared this reality with previous exercises and decided that the fire commander should, as he

The lookout at the Heugh battery.

effectively was now, always be knocked out early on in the game. Looking out from his post he was surprised to see a number of caps lying abandoned on the parade, blast from enemy shells had blown them from the heads of the busy gunners. Some unlucky gunners were even knocked from their feet as near misses rushed by.

> The shells they fired at us had delayed action fuses, so they hit the concrete, ricochetted over the top and exploded in the town. If the fuses had been instantaneous they would have burst as they struck the concrete, and probably destroyed us all, because there were two direct hits on the guns at the Heugh battery and one shell just cleared the front of the gun in Lighthouse Battery. (Sgt Major Pailor, ibid.)

Frustration was mounting at the Lighthouse. Time after time, the gun was reloaded only to misfire. Down in the magazines the men were well aware of the battle taking place, as echoes boomed around and the shells clanked together with each shudder. The noise rendered communication with the surface impossible and orders could not get through. Determined to play their part they doubled their efforts and sent shells and cartridges streaming up to the surface, unaware that the gun was broken. In all, it failed thirteen times but at last the cause was traced. A split pin was broken, causing the firing pin to miss. Makeshift repairs were carried out and another eight shells were fired, four of which hit their target. The gun captain, Jack Farmer, had been too busy with the repair work to notice the build-up of ammunition and it took a German shell ploughing into the earth and then bouncing just over their heads to draw his attention to the danger.

> We soon warmed to the job and it was not very long before the chain of action, from lifting the shell from the magazine to the actuation of the trigger was proceeding as smoothly as possible. When we changed from armour piercing shell to lyddite the gunners got so excited that they brought up scores of projectiles from the magazine and had them strewn all over the floor. I will always remember the look of disappointment on their faces when they were ordered to take them back.' (Sgt Major Pailor, ibid., p. 47)

The gun was now working well, the smoke had cleared and the *Blucher* had slowed down to present an almost stationary target. One round hit her, damaging some searchlight gear and aerials but Lieutenant Dickie Trenchmann was soon forced to order cease fire. As the ships moved north the gun's rotation came to a dead stop. Had the gun been able to traverse further the blast would have severely damaged the lighthouse.

> I can see Captain Jack Farmer smiling all over his face as the shells streamed steadily out of the guns without a hitch and then bursting violently into explosive words when the gun went out of action through being masked by the lighthouse. (Sgt Major Pailor, ibid.)

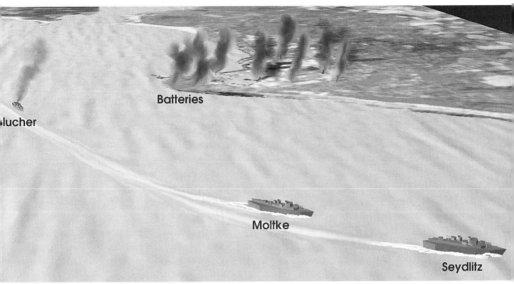

Seydlitz and Moltke steaming north.

For the next fifteen minutes or so, the Heugh guns continued their fire on the *Seydlitz*. An unwitting observer was John Horsley, a local fisherman who, aboard the coble *Children's Friend*, found himself caught in the crossfire. He noted many direct hits on the ships and was close enough to see that many of them simply bounced off. German fire was equally accurate but similarly ineffective: one shell landed directly in front of Heugh gun No. 2, only six feet from Gun Captain Mallin and bounced off the concrete apron, over his head, landing in the field behind and killing a donkey. The emplacement was hit again and, to Mallin's horror, the shell slewed to a halt by the ammunition lockers but fortunately it did not explode: 'At this time the noise was terrific and I have little more than a confused recollection of the din made by our guns and the enemy's bursting shells which were flying in fragments all around us.'

After about fifteen minutes of concentrated fire on the batteries, Seydlitz and *Moltke* disengaged and began slowly steaming northward, now aiming their fire into the town. At last Heugh gun No 2 came into the blast angle of gun No 1, the *Seydlitz* having moved out of the arc of fire. Following the fire plan, Captain Oscar Trenchmann, still on the parapet, used his megaphone to order change of target to the *Moltke*, but now to fire high explosive shells at her upper works. A few misses were observed as they found their range, then, as they saw the ships being hit, excitement rose. A gunner shouted out in encouragement, 'Go on shove 'em through! Shove 'em through! Give the buggers hell!' Patiently, Oscar Trenchmann reprimanded him, 'Do stop your dancing about and save your breath for your gun corrections' (M. Marsay, *Bombardment: The Day the East Coast Bled* (Great Northern Publishing, 1999)). After firing some twenty rounds at *Moltke*, the men found they were no longer under direct fire. At first relieved that the Germans appeared to be lousy shots, horror slowly dawned as they realized the ships were now targeting the docks and even firing into West Hartlepool.

The exception was *Blucher*, which took no part in the general bombardment but concentrated on keeping the batteries occupied. Nevertheless, she had also changed target to engage the rest of the coastal patrol, which was now struggling to leave the harbour. This was no easy task: to exit the Victoria Dock the cruisers and submarine had to negotiate a narrow angled channel, little longer than the vessels themselves, which could only be achieved by using tugs. Matters were made worse by the low tide, which caused more than one scrape on the bottom. As they made their exit, a randomly falling 11-in round struck HMS *Patrol*, killing four men and wounding seven others. Undaunted, *Patrol*, now free of by her tugs and cheered on by the guards at the Old Pier, pressed on, with Captain Bruce ordering full steam ahead. She managed to struggle past the harbour mouth, only to be hit by a second round, an 8.2-in from the *Blucher* which forced her to run aground. HMS *Forward*, following up behind, found her path blocked and was unable to progress further, leaving only submarine *C9* able to squeeze past and join the engagement. Her commander Lieutenant Dering was forced to dive to avoid being seen by the *Blucher* and slowly felt his way past the grounded Patrol. In only nine feet of water he managed to clear her to reach the open sea, scraping the bottom as he went. Remaining submerged in very poor visibility the submarine crew, when they finally surfaced, found they had lost direction and sailed too far south, arriving just off Seaton Carew.

Having neutralized the remainder of the coastal patrol, Blucher again changed target. Much to the bemusement of the gunners, her shells were now consistently falling short onto the tide-exposed rocks in front of the batteries and causing thick smoke to swirl across the shore. Her captain, believing that the Lighthouse gun had been knocked out, had ordered the firing of black powder shells in front of the Heugh Battery. He was in fact trying to blind the battery with a smokescreen in what is thought to be the first modern attempt at such a tactic. Struck by *Blucher's* strange behaviour, Captain Oscar Trenchmann realized that she was no longer being engaged by the Lighthouse gun. In fact, she was no longer weaving in the water but virtually stopped dead and firing unchallenged. The Heugh guns were immediately brought to bear and a change of ammunition ordered. Nineteen armour piercing shells were fired, but with little effect as the tired gunners struggled to work the autosights in the smoke, frequently having to stop through lack of visibility. Captain Trenchmann ordered a change back to high explosive aimed at the upper works, using Case II, which after a few misses seemed to have the desired effect, as *Blucher* disengaged and rapidly retired from the engagement, firing with her aft guns as she went.

Moltke and Seydlitz circled back from the north, firing towards Crimdon and the site of the old Cemetery Battery as they went. The retreating *Blucher* reached the bank of fog and safety and the gunners' aim was changed once again, with the final shells fired at the *Seydlitz*, now behind *Moltke*, following in the wake of the *Blucher*. The departing ships finally came back into the arc of fire of the Lighthouse gun and Gun Captain Jack Farmer's men managed to get off three last, electrically fired rounds before Lieutenant Dickie Trenchmann called a final cease fire. The Heugh guns continued to fire for a few more minutes until the *Seydlitz* began to slide into the mist. She was at a range of 9,500 yards when Captain Oscar Trenchmann stopped the gunners and checked his watch. The time was 8.53, thirty-eight minutes after the shelling had first started.

Silence descended on the batteries and Lieutenant Colonel Robson took a moment to look out of the small window at the back of the lookout. Everyone else had either been too occupied or not in a position to see what had been going on outside and he began to understand the effect of the bombardment. Columns of smoke peppered the town and flames from the burning gasometer rose starkly in the morning sky. Closer, he could see shattered houses and panicked civilians, some laden with possessions. Although the batteries had not suffered unduly, men had been lost and many others would be fearful for the safety of their families. He knew that this was a situation that would require considerable care and some tact to handle properly.

The effect of an 11-in shell at Victoria Place.

Oscar Trenchmann confirmed cease fire at the Heugh Battery and Bombardiers Malin and Hope congratulated their men, many now wondering how they had come through unscathed. Normality made an unexpected appearance with the arrival of refreshments, as Gunner Harry Tyson noted:

> I would like to say a word of praise to our cooks, Billy Sanderson and Arthur Hall. they must have been making tea all the time we were in action. As soon as we stopped firing out came the buckets full of hot tea. (Ward, Dawn Raid, p. 62)

Robson came down from the lookout and quietly spoke with Oscar Trenchmann. The guns were still loaded and were to be left that way. He did not expect the Germans to return but feared for the people of the town if they were to hear even more shots after this short lull. After a short rest some men were detailed to clear up the battery, while others were sent to help in the town. Many were to return to

The Heugh and Lighthouse gunners on the afternoon after the Bombardment.

the Lighthouse Battery later in the afternoon. Robson, with a well developed sense of occasion, lost no time in arranging a group photograph.

Once the men had been formed into workgroups and the clear up was under way the officers found time to write their respective reports on the action. Lieutenant 'Dickie' Trenchmann's was perhaps the most difficult to write, as it fell to him to explain why the Lighthouse Battery had had such appalling luck:

The Lighthouse Battery reported ready for action at 6:30 am The enemy's first broadside fired from 4,200 yards range struck many of the houses immediately behind Lighthouse Battery, and the smoke and dust from the explosions was so heavy that it was some minutes before it cleared away. There was very little wind. The enemy was engaged as soon as visible and the first round was fired at 4,500 yards. After the third round, which struck the forebridge, a misfire - tube not fired - occurred, subsequently found to have been caused by the 'A' lead having jumped at the rubbing contact. In order to carry on the engagement with as little delay as possible percussion fire was immediately resorted to. The rounds were then observed to be falling short, and correction ultimately had to be employed before further hits could be observed. Owing to the split pin below the adjustable bush under the catch, retaining LBM closed, having jarred loose or broken the lock dropped slightly, decentralising the needle, and 13 misfires occurred while the percussion method was in use. The spare lock was used after the first missfire (percussion) but with no better results. Subsequently the break in the circuit was found and remedied, and the last three rounds were fired electrically. All through the action the target was frequently obscured by smoke and dust from the enemies shells, and both DRF and layers were seriously hampered thereby. For the same reason observation of fire was rendered difficult, and hits were not easily recognised owing to the smoke of the ships' guns. 15 rounds were fired (10 by percussion, 4 electric); there were 13 percussion missfires and one electric these included 2 missfires 'tube fired'. HE Shell was used throughout with a view to attacking deck and superstructure. The megaphone was used for passing orders, and practically no difficulty was experienced, the BC's Post being close to the gun. The method of laying employed was Case II. Dials were checked after the action and found to be correct. The final range was 6,850 yards. Deflection had to be altered frequently and the target kept under careful observation as the ship was constantly manoeuvring to bring her different broadsides into play. The gun was put out of action before the enemy were outside effective range owing to the lighthouse coming into blast. (PRO WO 192/228, Lighthouse Battery, History of Work)

South Gare gunners after the Bombardment.

Following their retirement the German vessels sailed east to rendezvous with *Von der Tann* and *Derfflinger*, which were now heading north, having shelled Scarborough for the previous twenty minutes and killed nineteen civilians. As they passed Whitby at 9.00 am the Von der Tann and Derfflinger fired 200 rounds into Whitby, their main target being the coastguard signalling station. Fortunately, casualties were extremely light, with only three men killed. *Kolberg*, meanwhile, was returning from Filey where she had laid about a hundred mines and the six battleships of the reunited First Scouting Group began steaming at speed for Heligoland Bight at 9.30 am.

The first confirmation that an attack was under way had been received by the Admiralty at 8.19 am, when Lieutenant Commander Fraser sent his wireless signal from the stricken *Doon*. Further confirmation came from both Hartlepool and Scarborough at 8.40 am and signals were sent to Beatty and Warrender at Dogger Bank to intercept Hipper's group at the gap in the German minefield off Whitby. To prevent any escape to the north, eight pre-dreadnoughts carrying 12-in guns were sent south from Rosyth. It appeared that a trap had been well and truly set. Churchill, then First Lord of the Admiralty, was to write later:

Only one thing could enable the Germans to escape annihilation at the hands of an overwhelmingly superior force . . . The word 'Visibility' assumed a sinister significance. Warrender and Beatty had horizons of nearly ten miles . . . We went on tenterhooks to breakfast. To have this tremendous prize - the German battle-cruiser squadron whose loss would fatally mutilate the whole German Navy and could never be repaired - actually within our claws, and to have the whole event turn upon a veil of mist was a racking ordeal. (J Bullen, The German Battlecruiser Attack on the East Coast Ports (*Imperial War Museum, Journal, 1999*))

By 11.00 am the German and British forces were 100 miles apart and rapidly closing, so that within the next two and a half hours a clash seemed inevitable but, as Churchill feared, the weather intervened and reduced visibility down to about a mile. At 11.25 am outlying cruisers protecting the battlecruisers did make contact but confused semaphore signals caused the British cruisers *Southampton* and *Birmingham* to break off the action. The contact warned Hipper of the ambush and he ordered a change of course which, coupled with squalls of rain and banks of fog,

MOUTH

h Shields

DERLAND

HARTLEPOOL } Bombarded from 8.15 to 8.50 a.m
by 2 Battle CRUISERS &
WEST HARTLEPOOL } 1 Armoured CRUISER
Estimated about 500 Shells fired
91 Killed including 30 WOMEN & 15 CHILDREN
about 300 Wounded; Gasometer, Waterworks &
Towns much damaged

Carew
d

Tees Mouth

REDGAR

WHITBY to HARTLEPOOL 28 Miles

SALTBURN

HELIGOLAND NAVAL BASE to HARTLEPOOL 330 Nautical Miles or about
14 HOURS PASSAGE for a FAST CRUISER SQUADRON at 22-25 Knots

ESBROUGH

WHITBY Bombarded 9.15 to about 9.30 a.m.
by 2 Battle CRUISERS, about 30
shells fired; 2 Men killed, 2 Boys
wounded; Coastguard Sta. ABBEY,
Town & inland villages damaged

their average speed; th
journey can therefore
done under cover of NI

St Hilda's Church
WHITBY

The ABBEY
Shelled

RUSWARP
Shelled

EAST
CLIFF

River Esk

Eylingdale Moor

**ROBIN HOOD'S
BAY**

RAVENSCAR

Petard Point

SCALBY

NORTH BAY OLD CASTLE
Shelled

OLD CASTLE W
Damaged

St MARYS CHURCH
Hit

SHOP Set
on FIRE

SCARBOROUGH

OLD HARBOUR

NEW HARBOU
LIGHTHOU
Damaged

BALMORAL
HOTEL Hit

MANY HOUSES HIT in
this crowded quarter.

PROSPECT ROAD

HOUSES
Hit

HOUSES Hit

HANOVER

TOWN HALL

CAFÉ Struck

SOUTH BAY

GLADSTONE ROAD

VICTORIA

BARWICK

ROYAL HOTEL
Hit

HOUSE Hit

CRESCENT
RAILWAY STA.

WESTBOROUGH

GRAND HOTEL
Struck 3 times

FALSGRAVE ROAD

SCARBOROUGH
Bombarded from 8.5 to 8.25 a
by Battle CRUISER & Armoure
CRUISER, estimated about 3(
Shells fired; 17 KILLED inc
ing 8 WOMEN & 4 CHILDRE
about 100 Wounded

RAMSDALE PARK

VALLEY

ROAD

St MARTINS
CH. Damaged

SOUTH CLIFF
Shelled
PRINCE of WALES Hotel

Barbaric Kultur: German Navy's Bombardment of our East Coast Holiday resorts.

hid his movements from the British until he reached the safety of Heligoland. A last-ditch attempt to intercept his forces with submarines and destroyers off the mouth of the Jade was similarly foiled by the weather.

Hipper's escape was a cause of great anger in the Admiralty and prompted considerable censure by the press, who voiced dismay that the Navy had failed to save the towns. There was no satisfactory answer to the public's concern, as the Navy's actions could not be explained without revealing the role and secret nature of Room 40's code-breaking work. The frustration was to cause Admiral Beatty profound depression: 'If we had got them on Wednesday, as we ought to have done, we should have finished the war from a naval point of view' (quoted in R K Massie, *Castles of Steel* (Jonathan Cape, 2004), p. 355).

Probably the best view of the raid was seen from the cobles setting off for a day's fishing. Fortunately they were ignored by the German vessels and the only injury sustained was a broken leg when a fisherman jumped from his boat on reaching the shore. He was rescued by infantrymen manning the trenches at the old Cemetery Battery while shells flew overhead. Eyewitnesses commended the bravery of the infantrymen whom they thought to be under direct fire as they carried the wounded man to the shelter of the lifeboat house. Elsewhere, skipper John Horsley spent most of the action at sea and later made a slightly embellished statement of what he had seen:

I John Horsley of 21 Bedford St Hartlepool state that on Wednesday morning of the 16th December 1914 I proceeded to the sea in the fishing boat Children's Friend at about twenty minutes to eight. When we got outside we saw three ships flying the Union Jack and White Ensign. Just before that I saw the centre ship exchange signals with the lighthouse. They then hauled down the Union Jack and White Ensign and hauled up the German Flag. That was just before they opened fire on our Destroyers about two or three miles east-north-east of the German warships. There were four of our boats together, I turned about to come into Hartlepool but the other three boats ran ashore on the sands north of Hartlepool. Shortly after the leading ship fired on the batteries. Before they began firing at all the centre ship showed a red light at mast head which was answered by the other two with red lights. They fired at the batteries and the first shot from the Lighthouse Battery fell short, the second shot would have hit him but fell north. The next smashed on board and seemed to do some damage. I saw the shots from the battery hit the ships and as far as I could see very few of the battery shots missed. I saw some of the shots bounce off the ships sides and go into the air. At this time we were only half a mile from them. The crew had gone below and I called to see the way our guns were hitting the ships every time. When we were rounding the breakwater we saw the Patrol get hit. The submarine was alongside her a little to the north side. We ran inside the breakwater for three or four minutes. The shells commenced to fall about appeared to come over the battery. When we got as far as the Harbour opening about

A few unconsidered trifles, which failed to explode.

three minutes before the firing ceased we saw the Forward being towed out and cleared into West Hartlepool, to get out of her road. (Letter, author's collection)

This report, together with the initial confusion regarding the identity of the ships, seems to substantiate the rumour that the Germans had approached flying British flags but later it was admitted that this was not the case and the story downplayed.

Both towns at Hartlepool suffered severely during the attack, with 112 civilians killed outright or dying of their wounds later, and much damage was caused to property. It was recorded that the Germans ships fired just over 1,150 rounds and, although this figure may be on the high side, the raid was more devastating than the combined air raids the town was to suffer during both world wars. Probably the most significant damage was to the town's gasometer, causing a blaze that could be seen for miles and knocking out the town's lighting for a couple of days. Local industry suffered, with various workshops and pieces of plant being destroyed, while the timber merchants found much of their stock went up in smoke, but all were quick to recover. More lasting damage was done among the streets and houses and there were many stories of tragic incidents and miraculous escapes. John Davidson, who was starting work at the docks when the raid commenced, later wrote down his story of the attack:

At this time I was working in the engineering works of RWT Co. The first news was brought by the boy who delivered our morning paper. He told us 'The Germans are here.

Scene outside the wrecked Baptist chapel at West Hartlepool during the second Bombardment of our East Coast.

This we treated as a joke. But he had no sooner left us when we heard a rumbling noise, which gradually became louder. We then realised it was gunfire. We could hear the shells passing overhead and bursting in the factory. One putting the plant out of action. We now realised it was dangerous to stay at our posts and decided to investigate. On reaching the street, everybody was making for home. Curious to see what was really going on. We ran towards the sea front and plainly saw one of the German ships firing his broadsides in our direction. It was certainly time to seek shelter and get home as soon as possible. On coming down Princess St, Middleton we saw a shell strike the iron-dressing shop. Before we had gone 50 yards, a shell struck the corner of the general office. Pieces of shell and brickwork flying all around. Five men were killed at this point and others wounded. James Leighton, blacksmith was killed and his house at 16 Clifton Street was also hit. Another of the killed was Clayton Ramsey, pattern maker. A piece of shrapnel pierced the ear of Mr John Bell, turner.

A problem now arose, how to get home. Over the swing bridge to Hartlepool we were told was impassable. Our next choice was to try Middleton Road, this too we were warned was unsafe. We could see the gas-holder at Greenland blazing. Sheltering in Middleton Road we saw many shells drop into the Coal-dock. After about 20 minutes the firing ceased and we made for home via Arvour Terrace, Church Street and Hartlepool Road meeting droves of people leaving the town for shelter in the country. Passing over the dock gates, a man and young girl lay wounded. One shell pierced the interned German ship Ideneboah. A shell had just blown out the upper story of a house in Harbour Terrace, the bed was thrown into the roadway and feathers were flying all over. In their hurry to get home men had thrown away their tea and bait cans. At the foot of Church St a man and a newsboy lay dead. Just then the firing ceased it was 8.59 am. The electric tram wires had been cut, no trams available for Hartlepool. The telephone pole opposite the Mail Office was cut in two, the top portion dangling from the wires. In front of the Rink was a large crater, caused by a 12-in shell. A man lay dead and a doctor was ordering his removal.

The stream of folk from Hartlepool told us of great havoc in the town. Some of the people were scantily clad. The Scandinavian Church was badly scared and a shell had smashed the iron rails surrounding the water works. The Greenland gas-holder was still blazing having received a shell from one of the warships off Hart Station. The Tram offices had been hit and two houses were burning on the Central Estate. The upper storey of house in Percy Terrace was completely blown out. By this time motors and conveyances were racing to the Hartlepools Hospital with the wounded. The severest damage was in the vicinity of the batteries. Both St Hildas and St Marys churches received only slight damage. At St Marys the statue of the Blessed Virgin was untouched, only a slight portion of the niche was chafed. (Letter, author's collection)

It was the houses close by the batteries that suffered the most. Immediately behind the Lighthouse Battery was a café:, alongside Cliff House and Rockside, the residence of the Kay sisters, the first civilian casualties on mainland Britain. In 1915, local historian Frederick Miller wrote of the area:

Residential property in Moor Terrace and Victoria Place was well nigh wrecked. It was in Victoria Terrace that an officer of the Salvation Army, Adjutant William Avery lost his life. Two sisters, the Misses Kay, were killed in an upper room of their house in Cliff Terrace by a shell fired at the Lighthouse Battery. In this terrace, too, Miss Geipel was so seriously injured that she died a short time afterwards. The tenement house, 30

PROCLAMATION

NAVAL BOMBARDMENT

The Civil Population are requested as far as possible, to keep to their houses for the present. The situation is now secure.

The Group Leaders of each War will advise in case of further danger.

Any unexploded shells must not be touched, but information as to the position thereof given to the nearest Police Officer, or to the Police Station.

J. R. FRYER

Mayor.

Dated the 16th day of December, 1914.

GOD SAVE THE KING

William Street, was a veritable house of tragedy. The upper part of this house was the home of Mr and Mrs Dixon and their six children. Mr Dixon was away with Kitchener's Army at the time of the bombardment but his wife and children, seeking to escape from the house were struck down by an exploding shell. The mother was so maimed as to necessitate the amputation of a leg. She was unconscious for some days and is still' (12 Feb 1915) in hospital. Of her children three were killed and two injured...

But all around were harrowing scenes, taxing the nerve and skill of the brave ones who went to the rescue. Here an arm and part of a head had been blown off, here a young woman literally scattered in pieces, a poor woman riddled while gathering sea coal. (Miller, Under Shell Fire, p. 115)

A 5.9-in shell which failed to explode in Humphrey's shop.

While the attack was under way the Mayor summoned an emergency meeting of the War Emergency Committee and police and issued a proclamation which was printed and distributed within hours (ibid., p. 130):

The police, ambulance men and local volunteers all sprang into action to restore some order to the town and bring back those who were trying to escape. Shock seems to have blunted any panic that may have been expected and normal routine was soon established. The order not to touch unexploded shells was ignored in many cases and a thriving trade ensued, culminating in a profitable auction the following year. Only one person is thought to have died from this, having been hit by shrapnel while collecting fragments on a beach which was still under fire. Unfortunately, any semblance of normality gave way the following Friday, when an air raid warning was issued by Staff Captain Lyons. Miller described the result:

Somehow, Captain Lyons' poster was misread and misinterpreted. Word went round that the German ships were again in the bay and were about to renew their attack. This was straining distracted minds to breaking point. An industrial section of 70,000 souls threw down their tools, hurrying away, anywhere, from the German wrath to come. This was the saddest day in the town's history. Again the morning was only half awake. Mothers snatched hold of their children and raced for the park, the byways and hedges. The staff at the railway station could hardly cope with the rush for trains. At York on the evening of this sorrow stricken day, would be passengers to the Hartlepools were told that it was doubtful if they would get through. (Ibid., p. 132)

During the attack 33 civilians had been killed on the Headland and 46 at West Hartlepool. Many others died later from the injuries they had received and the final figure rose to 112: 51 on the Headland and 61 at West Hartlepool. These comprised 43 men, 32 women and 37 children (F. Miller, *The Hartlepools in the Great War* (Sage Bookseller & Stationer, 1920)).

The day after the attack, the gunners were assembled at fortress command in West Hartlepool, where they paraded in front of General Plumber, the officer commanding Northern Command. He addressed them and read out a letter of congratulation he had received that morning from Lord Kitchener. They were then marched around the Headland so that they could see the extent of the damage.

The recess in front of the Heugh Battery was furrowed with deep trenches. The trajectory of the shells had been so low that they cut horizontal grooves in the ground, right up to the walls of the Batteries. (W. Boagey in Ward, Dawn Raid, p. 73)

In 1916 when the Military Medal was instituted, the first two were awarded to the Heugh Battery gun captains Sergeant F W Mallin and Acting Bombardier J J Hope for their part in the Bombardment. The Distinguished Conduct Medal went to Sergeant T Douthwaite for removing the live cartridge from the Lighthouse gun.

Lieutenant Colonel Robson continued to serve as fire commander throughout the war and continued to be one of the main instigators of changes in the Hartlepool and Tees defences. For his part in the Bombardment he was made a Companion of the Distinguished Service Order and in 1917 the Companion of the Order of St Michael and St George was presented to him by the King. Following promotion to colonel in August 1918 he retired from the army to continue his work for Hartlepool Council. Previously, in 1908, he had held the position of mayor.

Captain Oscar Trenchmann left the battery with many other gunners in 1915 to join 41 Siege Battery in France and returned to replace Robson as fire commander in 1918 on his final retirement. In all, the Durham Royal Garrison Artillery raised 85 officers and 2,000 other ranks for service overseas. Although proud of this achievement, a running joke amongst the veterans was that 'it was a bit thick to have taken on the German Navy and then proceed overseas and get it all over again from the Army' (Durham RHA Scrapbook 1856-1938, D/DLI6/1/6).

Although the seamen of the coastal patrol did not receive any awards, perhaps because of criticism levelled at the Navy for failing to prevent the attack, their efforts were appreciated by the townsfolk who expressed their gratitude:

The Committee representing the tradesmen of the Hartlepool and District Traders Defence Association thereby express their admiration of the gallant conduct of the Officers and Men of His Majesty's ships stationed at Hartlepool in so bravely going out to engage the enemy who were in such overwhelming force...Their conduct has fully maintained the best traditions of the British Navy. (Bullen, *German Battlecruiser Attack*, p. 103)

Hartlepool's coastal patrol were soon dispersed to other ports, with the cruisers going to the Humber in 1915, but by then town's defences had been supplemented by a monitor armed with a 12-in gun. To speed up her deployment she was placed under Lieutenant Colonel Robson's direct control while in port, reverting to Admiralty command at sea. By the end of war the cruisers and destroyers were surplus to requirements and all went to the breaker's yard, HMS *Forward* being the last in 1921.

The effects of a 5.9-in shell at Grovenor Street, West Hartlepool.

SMS *Seydlitz* and *Moltke*, along with *Von der Tann* and *Derfflinger* survived the war to be scuttled in Scapa Flow in 1918. *Moltke* and *Von der Tann* were involved in a further raid at Lowestoft on 25 April 1916 while *Seydlitz* was damaged during the Battle of Dogger Bank and almost sunk at the Battle of Jutland, where she was hit twenty-two times. The older and slower Blucher was less fortunate. Following repair for damage inflicted during the Bombardment, she was sunk at the Battle of Dogger Bank on 24 January 1915.

That the batteries at Hartlepool did not act as an effective deterrent is hardly surprising, given that the guns were not capable of penetrating the battlecruisers' armour. Superstructure and to a lesser extent gun turrets were vulnerable but the main armour belt was impenetrable. Eyewitness accounts of shells bouncing off the sides of the ships, coupled with deficiencies in British ammunition found later at Jutland, suggest that many of the shells fired by the batteries may well have been duds. The Germans reported three hits on *Seydlitz*, one on *Moltke* and four on *Blucher*, which suffered the worst damage, but the accounts suggest that far more

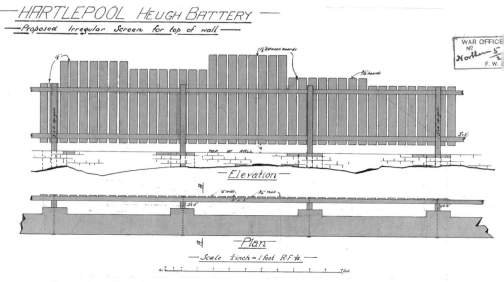

Camouflage fence intended to create the effect of a raised skyline.

rounds found their target but were not recorded as they caused no damage.

German fire was accurately targeted on the batteries, probably greatly assisted by using the lighthouse as an aiming mark and direct hits were inflicted on both. Heugh gun No. 2 and the Lighthouse gun both would most likely have been destroyed had the Germans not used time delay fuses which caused the shells to bounce of the emplacements and over the batteries before exploding. The choice of fuse was deliberate, with the intention that the shells would bury their way toward the magazines and would have been more effective had the range and angle of fall been greater. The overshooting was also made worse by the camouflage screen erected at the back of the Heugh at Robson's insistence, which took the form of wooden planks laid out to create a false skyline. Undoubtably it protected the battery, although at least four 11-in shells exploded within fifty yards of the battery command post and several 5.9-in hit the aprons, but at the expense of the housing behind. Captain Oscar Trenchmann recognized the detrimental effect of the batteries being so close to a residential area in his report of the event:

> I believe the enemy must have fired about 1000 rounds, many of these directed at West Hartlepool, where considerable damage was done to property and many lives lost. Hartlepool also suffered badly, but most of this, to my mind, was done by shots which were directed on the battery. (PRO WO 192/228, History of Bombardment)

Militarily, the worst damage was caused by the first shell which destroyed the telephone lines, isolating Robson, the fire commander. However, the ships were easily visible and by shouting their orders through megaphones the battery

BOMBARDMENT OF THE HARTLEPOOLS

16th DECEMBER, 1914.

MR. I. J. ROBINSON, F.A.I.

WILL SELL BY AUCTION,

AT 2-30 P.M.,

On Tuesday, 16th March, 1915,

AT BIRKS' CAFE, WEST HARTLEPOOL,

Pieces, Noses, Bases, Copper Bands, Screw Heads, Fuse Boxes and Caps, of Highly Explosive German Shells,

FROM 1 lb. TO 96 lbs IN WEIGHT,

(Collected by Mr. JOHN ATKINSON, Tailor.)

ON VIEW FROM 9 A.M. ON SALE DAY.   TERMS: CASH.

After the Bombardment there was a roaring trade in souvenirs.

commanders were able to control the guns effectively. Paradoxically, the bank of fog worked in favour of the batteries by bringing the battlecruisers much closer to the shore, enabling the use of autosights, which were surprisingly effective given they were being used just within their maximum calibrated range of 4,256 yards.

One problem immediately came to light: the lighthouse limited the traverse of the Lighthouse gun and seriously obscured the view from the Heugh. In fact, the situation had been officially recognized as far back as 1883 but as it stood outside the battery boundary the issue had not been pushed. It was immediately pulled down and a temporary light erected on the Town Moor. Behind the Lighthouse Battery a café, Cliff House and Rockside, all shattered by shellfire were demolished in 1915 and Bath Terrace moved back to make more room for the Lighthouse Battery

The number of miss-fires suffered by all three guns is striking but does not appear as a cause of concern in the official reports which, combined with Robson's high regard for the efficiency of his batteries, suggests that such problems were to be expected with coast defence guns.

It has been argued that, had the remainder of the coastal patrol, particularly the submarine, been at sea, the outcome might have been very different. I suggest that this is idle speculation. There is no reason why the light cruisers would not have

Plaque marking the spot where the first gunners were killed.

been brushed aside as easily as the destroyers long before they could get into torpedo range, while the submarine was so slow that she would have been extremely lucky to get into position without being spotted. We must also take into account that neither the U-boats deployed off the Humber nor British submarines sent to ambush the battlecruisers at the Jade had any effect on the outcome of the action.

Regardless of the risk to the High Seas Fleet, coastal raiding did not fall out of favour, though it took second place to air raids by Zeppelin and aircraft as the war progressed. The next raid took place on 16 August 1915, when the coast of Cumberland was bombarded, but with no damage caused or casualties inflicted. A larger attack took place when Great Yarmouth received her second visit on 25 April 1916 during a combined operation of battlecruisers and Zeppelins against Yarmouth and Lowestoft, leaving four dead. Again this was led by Hipper and included *Moltke* and *Von der Tann*. Historically, the most important raid was to take place on 31 May 1916 when Sunderland was to be attacked, but it was aborted at the last minute in favour of a sweep of the North Sea, leading to the most important sea battle of the war at Jutland. On 12 July 1916 there was a change in tactics when a U-boat reluctantly shelled Seaham. It is said that the captain, knowing the town from before the war, deliberately fired wide into the colliery pit yard but unfortunately one woman was killed. Given the small calibre of the gun, this was little more than a nuisance raid. However, on the same night, a submarine sank three armed trawlers off the Scottish coast. November 1916 saw more light raiding, with a raid in the English Channel on the 23rd and another armed trawler sunk of Great Yarmouth on the 26th. In 1917 the focus shifted to the South coast, with ineffective raids at Southwold on 25 January and Dover on 20 March. Two people were then killed during a night time raid at Ramsgate and Broadstairs. Scarborough was to receive a second visit on 4 September 1917, when shells fired by a U-boat killed three people, and Great Yarmouth received her fourth visit on 14 January 1918, when six people were killed. The final raid of the war came on 15 February 1918, when a U-boat paid a last visit to Dover, killing one person.

I leave the final words to Frederick Miller, an inhabitant of Hartlepool who wrote two books on the role played by Hartlepool during the Great War. He was under no doubt as to why the German raid had been so effective:

Few will now doubt that inside the shore line, from Hart to Seaton, from the end of the breakwater to the confines of Elwick, we were infested with an ants nest of spies. We can recall most of them now. (The Hartlepools in the Great War (Sage Bookseller & Stationer, 1920))

Table of Military Casualties at Hartlepool

Royal Garrison Artillery

Gunner William Houston, Gunner Robert Spence

Royal Engineers

Sapper Little

18th Durham Light Infantry

Corporal Alex Liddle, Lance Corporal C S Clark, Private Theo Jones, Private Les Turner, Private Walter Rogers, Private Tom Minks 11 other members of the DLI were wounded. The first soldier killed is generally claimed to have been Theo Jones but it could have been Liddle, Clark or Turner, all of whom were hit by the first shell.

HMS Patrol

Leading Seaman R W Hook, Armourers Crew G C Martin, Able Seaman E C Cummings (lost overboard), ERA 1st Class P J Sheridan (died of wounds). Four seamen were also wounded.

HMS Doon

Stoker 1st Class James Fraser.
Another 11 seamen were wounded.

GAZETTEER

This chapter details all batteries known in the Tyne, Tees and Humber regions between 1860 and 1956. Please be aware that much research still needs to be done and there are bound to be omissions and mistakes. The Hartlepool defences are described in greater detail, due to the role they played in the Bombardment, but many of their features can be seen at other sites. Batteries are grouped by the defended ports as they were defined between 1905 and 1956. So, for example, Scarborough appears under the Tees defences. They are nominally listed running down the coast from north to south.

Also included are details of submarine mine depots and those Volunteer practice batteries that have been traced. Grid references, where known, are given. No attempt has been made to catalogue the numerous barracks and drill halls associated with the defences.

For those who would like to visit the sites a system of stars has been used. Where no star is given the site has disappeared completely or at least no evidence on the ground has been noted. As many of these were simply buried it is likely that magazines and parts of the emplacements remain for the future archaeologist.

*** The site is protected, actively maintained and open to the public.
** There are significant remains.
* Not much remains to be seen or what does is hard to interpret.

The recommended top five sites for the casual visitor are, from north to south:

Blyth Battery, Northumberland
Tynemouth Castle
Heugh Battery, Hartlepool
Spurn Fort, Humberside
Fort Paull, Humberside

Some of the sites open to the public have websites which are worth checking for opening times and activities. Lastly, a word of caution: a number of batteries are above dangerous cliffs while others are hazardous, especially in the magazine sections. Accidents do happen and people have been killed while illicitly visiting derelict military sites. Be warned and be safe. If in doubt of rights of way to a site, approach the owner. Never trespass as this endangers yourself and only makes future access more difficult.

TYNE DEFENCES

In 1899 Montgomery wrote:

> The object of an enemy approaching the Tyne would be to destroy the Elswick Works (which are at once the most important private ordnance factory and one of the most important dockyards in the kingdom) and also to destroy the Jarrow and other shipbuilding establishments. We do not consider therefore that this can be treated merely as a commercial port.

However, by 1905, Tynemouth was downgraded to being liable to 'C class attack' and by blockers only.

Tyne defences.

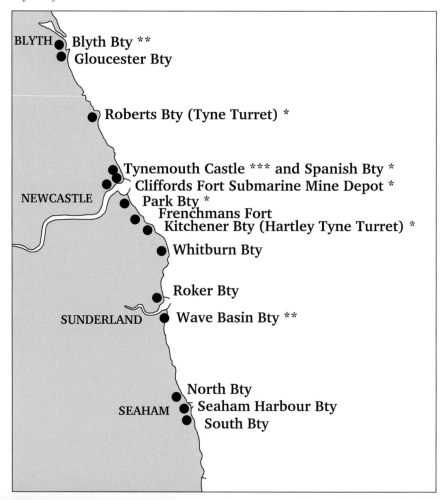

Holy Island Volunteer Practice Battery

Lindisfarne Castle was built as a two-battery gun fort between 1565 and 1571. One platform was used in the 1890s by the Lindisfarne Artillery Volunteers for three 64pr RML. The castle is open to the public and the racers for the guns can still be seen.

Druridge Battery

A Second World War emergency battery for two 6-in guns on 15 degree mountings.

Blyth Battery 1916-45 **
NZ 321:793

Blyth Battery, also known as Fort Coulson, Link House Battery and Seaton Battery, was built during the First World War to protect the nearby submarine base at Blyth Harbour. It was one of the first 6-in batteries to be purpose-built for searchlights. Construction began in August 1916 and the battery was handed over by Durham Royal Engineers in February 1918 under the name of Fort Coulson. The site was split in two sections, with guns and observation posts to the south and searchlights and engine room to the north. The two guns were mounted in the standard configuration, with the underground magazine between them and a shelter with rooms for the gunners, officers and battery sergeant major was placed behind them. Just north of the guns a two-storey BOP comprised a telephone room on the ground floor and BCP and director's post above. A Barr and Stroud rangefinder was mounted on top. When first built, three pillboxes were added for ground defence and the searchlight emplacements had loopholed walls

Blyth Battery: the searchlights are a few yards north of this site.

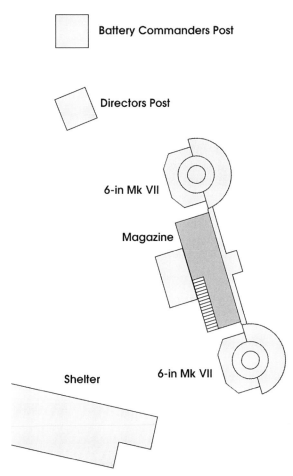

built to the same design as the existing loopholed latrine at Roberts Battery

The battery was decommissioned after 1918, with parts being incorporated into the beach amenities, and the engine room became a toilet.

It was reactivated in 1940 when a second post was added containing a battery plotting room and the area fire command post for 510 Coast Regiment. New 6-in guns were fitted and the emplacements modified, with the addition of overhead covers to protect against aerial attack. It is thought that the change of name to Seaton Battery took place at this time. It was recommended for upgrading to 5.25-in CD/AA but the work was not carried out.

The battery remains in good condition, is open to the public and has Listed Building status. The local council is currently considering restoring the site and a survey has been undertaken. Restoration costs are estimated at around £170,000 (2003).

Gloucester Battery * NZ 323:784

A Second World War counter-bombardment battery armed with two 6-in Mk XXII guns. The site was completed and ready for action on 6 June 1940. Little remains and the bases of the emplacements are usually only visible after winter storms.

Roberts Battery (Hartley Tyne Turret) * NZ 342:762

As a result of the Bombardment of Hartlepool it was decided to build Roberts Battery at Hartley and Kitchener Battery at Marsden to protect the Tyne approaches. Initially it was hoped to mount American 14-in guns on HP carriages but a delivery time of three years was quoted and plans were drawn up for 13.5-in naval turrets instead. It was then found that the barrels would not fit the existing turrets and an alternative was sought. HMS *Illustrious* had formed part of the coast patrol on the Tyne and the Navy, wishing to convert her to an ammunition store, offered up her turrets and these were accepted in desperation. A single turret was fitted at each battery. These are the only examples of complete ex-warship turrets emplaced anywhere in the British Empire. The advantage of using a complete turret was that the mountings, motors and most of the ammunition train were already included. Emplacement would have been far more difficult had only barrels been provided. The guns were 12-in Mk VIII dated to 1895 and were considered obsolete by the Navy as newer guns could be reloaded at any elevation. These had to be levelled to be loaded and the rate of fire was slow, at only one round every forty-two seconds. Although they provided a useful increase in the Tyne's defences the guns actually had a shorter range than the existing 9.2-in.

Work commenced in 1917 and was completed in September 1921 at a cost of £64,000. Peacetime and post-war cutbacks meant that the turrets were never manned full-time. In fact, when it came to proof firing, the army used cooks as part of the crew as they were so short of men. The batteries were only active for five years and dismantling began in April 1926, probably because the guns were non-standard and spares unobtainable. Nevertheless, the batteries outlived the

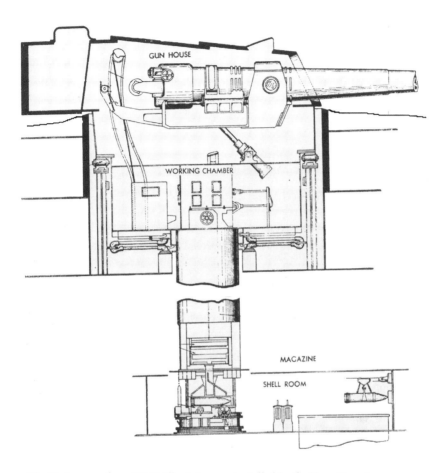

The 12-in guns from HMS Illustrious as installed in the Tyne Turrets.

Illustrious, which was scrapped in 1920.

The emplacement and underground works contained the usual magazines and stores, along with an engine room and control gear for the turret. The BOP, mounting a 30 foot Barr and Stroud rangefinder, stood alongside accommodation and stores and was situated to the south surrounded by a loopholed wall.

The gun site has been levelled, leaving only a circular depression in the ground, but the BOP and other buildings, including a defensible latrine, survive at the property now known as Fort House which is a Grade II Listed Building. The pillbox built into the loopholed wall is a rare surviving example from the First World War. Other visible remains around the site are from a Second World War AA searchlight battery and a Chain Home Low radar station. The site is accessible.

Kitchener Battery (Marsden Tyne Turret) NZ 397:656

Tynemouth Castle as it is today.

An identical battery to Roberts Battery with the same history. During the Second World War there was an AA battery about 400 yards behind the site and it is recorded that four soldiers were injured during an air raid when a shell fired from a gun burst on the night of 9 April 1941.

Tynemouth Castle *** NZ 385:694

The Headland at Tynemouth is an important historical site, having been the site of an early Christian monastery, a later priory and defences dating back to at least 1095. The original artillery defences date to 1544 but these had fallen into ruination by 1676. The Napoleonic Wars led to the building of new batteries, which at their height held thirty-two 18pr, eight 12pr and eleven 9pr.

The castle was used by Armstrong for gun trials in 1867 and also served as a depot for a large number of smoothbore guns going to Elswick for reboring to RML. The deep trench on the landward side is the remains of a quarry used for the construction of the piers in 1886. There were plans to fill it in in the 1930s but the army argued that it should stay as most castles had a moat!

In 1877 recommendations were made to upgrade the smoothbores to 10-in RML and by 1881 there were six RML with twenty older smoothbores on site.

Breech loaders were introduced in 1893, when two 6-in Mk VI on HP mount were fitted, and in the following year the last pair of 64pr RML were replaced by two 12pr QF guns covering the entrance to the Tyne. The 6-in HP guns were removed in 1901 and a new set of emplacements and magazines constructed for a pair of 6-in Mk VII. A single 9.2-in Mk X on Mk V mounting was added in 1904 and two 6pr guns were brought into the battery for training. In 1902 Villiers House, which stood just behind the gun line, was demolished and a new BCP, director's post and DRF post built on the site. Searchlights stood at the

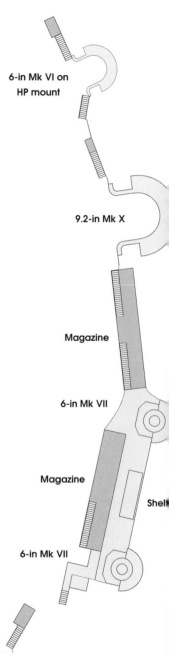

6-in Mk VI on HP mount

9.2-in Mk X

Magazine

6-in Mk VII

Magazine

Shell

6-in Mk VII

12pr Battery

foot of the cliff and worked in conjunction with those at South Shields. By 1905 the 9.2-in and 12pr were considered superfluous and the 12pr were removed in 1910. The 9.2-in was allowed to remain 'for drill', and remained in service until the middle of the Second World War. In 1940 a 4-in gun was also placed at the site of the present heliograph to train the crews of defended merchant ships.

Tynemouth Castle and the nearby Spanish Battery became a regular venue for Northern Command summer camps after the First World War. Here men from other areas were trained in the latest methods of coast defence and were able to familiarize themselves with the 9.2-in gun which by the mid-1930s had earned the nickname 'Old Bess'.

Tynemouth Castle acted as the hub of the Tyne defences during both world wars and continued working until disbandment in 1956. It was used during the Second World War for experiments in using infra red to detect shipping in poor weather conditions. This was a promising line of research, but was largely abandoned when radar was introduced.

The battery is well worth a visit. For the casual visitor there is the castle and priory while the artillery enthusiast will find the best selection of emplacement types in the region. Unfortunately, all the smaller and temporary buildings apart from the master gunners residence were removed when the army vacated the site. The observation posts were also removed in the 1980s to make way for the new coastguard station. Nevertheless, the extensive post-1893 gun lines have all survived and have been renovated along with magazines, workshops and shelters.

The gun lines from north to south comprise a two-gun 6-in Mk VI HP battery, with one emplacement buried and the other converted to a Second World War store; a 9.2-in Mk X emplacement, the site of 'Old Bess'; a two-gun 6-in Mk VII battery in very good condition and, overlooking the Tyne, a two-gun 12pr battery.

A 6-in Mk 23 has even been installed in the Mk VII battery which, while not correct, gives a very good impression of how the guns looked. Further weapons displayed on site include a 32pr smoothbore, a naval 4-in and mount, a 4.7-in mount, two 5.25-in barrels, a 3.7-in AA gun and a 5.5-in field gun. At the time of writing, negotiations were under way to transfer some of this equipment to the Heugh Battery for renovation.

The site belongs to English Heritage and is open throughout the year, although the magazines can only be visited during summer. A guidebook is available.

Spanish Battery * NZ 374:691

Originally built in 1545 as part of the outer defences of Tynemouth Castle, the battery is thought to take its name from the Spanish mercenaries quartered here during preparations for an invasion of Scotland in 1544. Originally a two-tier stone revetted gun platform, it was improved during the English Civil War before falling into decay. The site was chosen by the Inspector General of Fortifications to cover the entrance to the Tyne in 1854 with smoothbores. In 1877 recommendations were made to upgrade the smoothbores to 10-in RML, modified to two 6-in guns and one 9.2-in gun. The battery was upgraded for breech loaders in 1893 and mounted

Although not entirely correct, this 6-in Mk 23 gives a good impression of how the guns looked.

two 6-in guns on HP mounts facing seaward, with two 12pr mounted at right angles covering the river entrance. The HP guns were replaced in 1901 and the original emplacements reworked for 6-in Mk VII guns and, with the addition of a searchlight, it was used as the examination battery. The DRF located just behind the 6-in guns had been replaced by a Barr and Stroud rangefinder by 1938.

The battery was used as part of the training facilities at Tynemouth Castle and was regularly occupied by visiting regiments.

The BCP and all ancillary buildings have been removed and the whole landscaped. The concrete aprons and retaining wall top for both the 6-in and 12pr positions remain uncovered and are presently used as platforms for benches. The site is open to the public and stands by a car park which serves Tynemouth Castle.

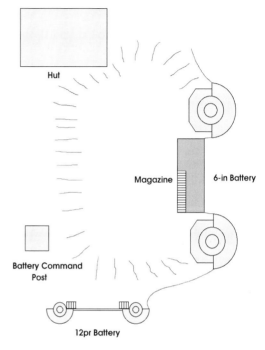

Spanish Battery.

Cliffords Fort and Submarine Mine Depot * NZ 364:685

Originally built for smoothbores to cover the inner entrance of the Tyne, the site was strongly constructed with a substantial stone wall pierced with embrasures on the seaward side and barracks within. In 1861 a number of families were living here: Master Gunner John Knox with his wife and six children, along with the families of a sergeant, bombardier, two gunners and a foreman. It was recommended for upgrading to 10-in RML in 1877 but this does not seem to have been carried out. By 1893 the new piers across the mouth of the Tyne obstructed the field of fire and the battery was declared obsolete. The site was converted to a submarine mine depot and equipped with searchlights, two 6pr QF guns and two Maxim guns and operated by the Tyne Division Volunteers until 1907. When the miners disbanded, the site appears to have been closed down. During the Second World War an emergency battery for two 12pr was built on the quayside in front of the fort.

The area is now part of a run-down industrial estate and at present little remains to be seen. The council who own the fort are currently in the process of tidying up the site and restoring the original embrasures and as a result the 6pr positions are again visible. Most of the site is on private land but areas can be viewed and there is a car park close by.

A Company, Tyne Submarine Miners in 1895.

Frenchman's Point Battery

In 1894 one 9.2-in gun and two 6-in guns were approved for the site but no work was carried out until September 1902 when 6-in Mk VII guns were fitted. There was some dispute about the usefulness of the site, as in 1905 Owen declared it redundant, but in 1907 the recommendations were to keep the 'fine modern armourment of this work'. It was closed in 1912 only to be reinstated in 1914 when it was hastily manned by a company of Durham RGA and administered from Hartlepool. Fieldworks were dug around site during the First World War. The site was sold after war and used as a holiday camp.

An emergency battery was built on the site in 1940 for two 6-in guns but these were removed for use at Park Battery in early 1941. Three 7.5-in Mk VI guns were then fitted in concrete emplacements and remained in place until closure in 1943, when the Park Battery rebuild was completed. This was a rather unusual choice of gun, having been introduced for trade protection vessels in 1919. Only forty-four guns were made as they were found to be cumbersome and difficult to use. Seventeen were transferred for coast defence but these were the only guns mounted in Britain, the remainder going to Canada, the Dutch West Indies and Mozambique.

The site has been partially demolished and landscaped. Emplacement A1 was removed but A2 remains buried under a grassy mound. A coast artillery searchlight also stands at 383:666.

Park Battery (South Shields) * NZ 368:678

Originally built in 1940 as Devon Emergency Battery for two 6-in guns and manned by the Royal Marines. The Marines left in 1941 when replacement 6-in guns were transferred from Frenchman's Point Battery. In 1943 it was upgraded for the CD/AA role and was unique as it was the only British battery ever to mount

5.25-in guns. There were proposals to mount the same guns at Falmouth and Southsea Castle at Portsmouth but the only other places where they were actually fitted were in one battery at Malta and two at Gibraltar. The guns covered the entrance to the Tyne and stood between the piers and, although they had a good field of fire to the front, they were restricted by housing close behind.

The battery has been levelled and is now parkland. Some buried traces are just visible. One building in the park is thought to be associated with the Tyne Turrets.

Whitburn Battery

There was a Volunteer practice battery at Trow Point, containing two 64pr RML for use by the Durham Volunteer Artillery. Later, two 6-in Mk VII on 15 degree mountings were installed which went into care and maintenance in 1944. Whitburn was well known to the Durham and Tynemouth Territorials as it was here that most small arms training took place and the ranges continue to be used by local Territorials today. Some holdfasts survive but are threatened by coastal erosion.

Abb's Point Battery/Roker Battery NZ 406:593

In 1894 three 64pr RML were emplaced here and there was a proposal to replace them with 6-in guns. By 1905 they had been removed. Although 6-in Mk VII were recommended, Sunderland entered the First World War without guns. Two 4.7-in guns were finally emplaced here in 1917. During the Second World War two 6-in guns were fitted. The site was intended to be upgraded to 5.25-in CD/AA. Two emplacements are visible but the remainder has been landscaped.

Seaham Battery

A Second World War emergency battery built between the piers containing two 6-in Mk VII.

North Battery, Seaham NZ 427:501

Originally situated halfway down the cliff, just north of Featherbed Rock, this Volunteer practice battery originally mounted four 32pr on garrison carriages standing on simple rectangular platforms with a small side arm store at the north end. An old boat was tied up by Featherbed Rock to serve as a target. Another target, used for Snyder rifle practice, was placed on the south side of the rock but this was considered unsafe when the Martini Henry was introduced. Unlike South Battery, the land did not belong to the military and the usual War Department boundary stones are not shown on maps.

A café was built on the abandoned site in 1923, by which time the platforms were crumbling into the sea and nothing now remains. Coastal erosion and quarrying has also affected Featherbed Rock, which is now substantially smaller than in the 1890s.

South Battery, Seaham NZ 433:485

This battery was located on War Department land and appears to have formed part of the town's defences, being equipped with four 64pr RML. It was later relegated to use as a Volunteer practice battery.

Wave Basin Battery, Sunderland ** NZ 410:581

The site was given in 1860 by River Wear Commission to the War Office. Four emplacements for 80pr RML were built on the mole projecting into the river inside the harbour. It was not considered for upgrading to BL guns as the site was too small and replacement sites were examined around the North Pier and south towards Hendon. A submarine mining depot was also recommended but not built. By 1894 the battery was used for practice only.

This is the only surviving example of an RML battery between the Humber and the Tweed.

Roker Battery, Sunderland

During the First World War Sunderland was unprotected until the town was shelled by U-boat in 1917. Roker Battery was then built for two 4.7-in guns. During the Second World War, two 6-in guns were fitted. It was recommended for upgrading to 5.25-in CD/AA but the work was not carried out.

Barrons Battery, Sunderland

A Second World War emergency battery for two 12pr guns.

HARTLEPOOL AND TEES DEFENCES

'This is a commercial port. The object of its defence is the same as that of any other purely commercial port, viz, to defeat the raiding attack of cruisers which may have eluded the vigilance of the fleet, and might attack for the purpose of destroying merchant shipping and other accessible property of value.' (Montgomery, 1899)

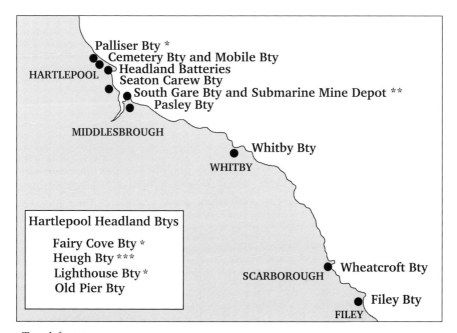

Tees defences.

Palliser (Hart Warren) Battery * NZ 505:356

In 1917 it was decided to supplement the Hartlepool and Tees defences with two 9.2-in Mk X guns on Mk VI 30 degree high angle mountings, one to be placed at the north of Hartlepool in Palliser Battery, with the other at the mouth of the Tees in Pasley Battery. These were the only single-gun batteries of this type. Work began at Palliser in 1918, to be completed three years later when the gun was proof fired in August 1921.

A single 63 foot diameter emplacement occupied the centre of the site, with separate underground cartridge and shell stores just to the south. Shells were transported between the magazine and gun on rail trollies. The magazine complex held the usual small lamp room and a dressing station. The shell and cartridge stores were parallel with lamp niches running the length of the dividing wall: even

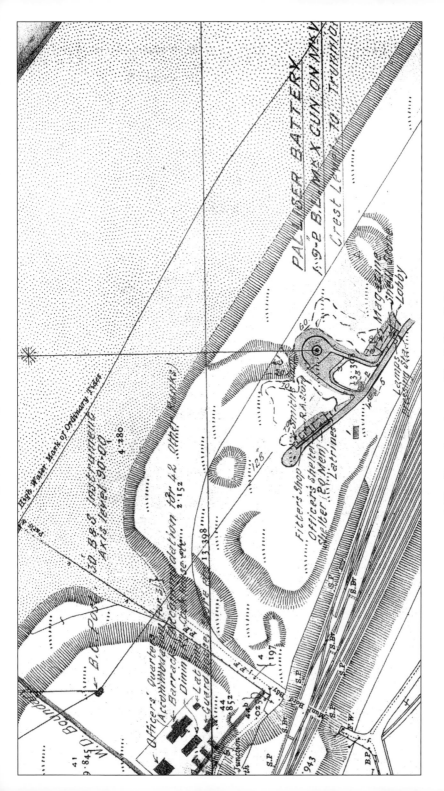

A War Department map of the Palliser Battery.

at this late date candles were still the approved illumination. Close by the gun were all the facilities needed for minor repairs, the RA store and smiths and fitters shops. Also to the rear stood a shelter for twenty men and a latrine.

The main services for the battery stood well away from the gun at the northern end of the site. Here a total of five buildings and three huts were erected, the largest being a barracks for forty-two men. Quarters for officers were also provided, along with dining room and cookhouse, a guardhouse and latrine standing on a rectangular parade. Also in the northern section was the BCP housing a 30 foot Barr and Stroud rangefinder complemented with a position finder receiver post to the south of the battery.

The War Department purchased the northern parcel of land in early 1924 but were unable to acquire the remainder of the site which was leased from North East Railways. Unable to agree a reasonable notice to quit, the War Department withdrew and closed the battery in 1928, although the northern section remained in military hands until sold to Steetly Magnasite in 1957.

Little remains to be seen of the battery, which has been built over by a magnasite works. The magazines are accessible and in surprisingly good condition, although some modifications for a later small bore rifle club are evident. Under the magazine parapet is a biographical plaque to General Palliser, the Napoleonic general after whom the battery was named. Some of the buildings in the northern section remain in varying conditions, having been incorporated into the works. There is no public access to this highly industrialized site.

Cemetery Battery NX 511:349

As there was no constraint on the site nor any old fabric to demolish, the latest designs could be employed for this battery. Construction began on 1 May 1893 and was completed on 23 June 1894 at a total cost of £5,060 for two 6-in Mk IV guns on Mk II hydro pneumatic mounts.

The site was enclosed by a thick earth embankment 20 feet high, and surrounded by a 9 foot high palisade (unclimbable fence). Two emplacements were constructed with a magazine between containing a separate shell and cartridge store for each gun. Above the magazine a parapet ran between the guns to an open BCP. By the side of each gun stood a separate pit for rangefinding equipment. An underground latrine and small guardroom completed the battery. Just outside the battery compound, set on its own small plot of land, stood a master gunner's quarters.

Due to its location, it was not considered worthy of upgrading when the 6-in Mk VII was introduced. The Montgomery Committee of 1899 would have seen the battery closed but 'as we believe it does not require any garrison of regular troops we think it may as well be kept up for the sake of moral effect, not on the enemy, but on the inhabitants of Hartlepool'. It was too far north to add much to the defence of the harbour and too distant from the fire commander's post at Fairy Cove to be effectively controlled. As an interim measure, a fire commander's post and new position finder were built on site in 1904 but it was finally abandoned in

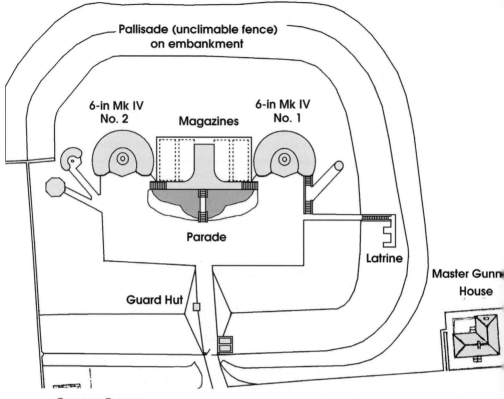

Cemetery Battery.

1907.

The site was later used for a Bofors light AA battery before being built over by industry and is inaccessible. An unused section of the original War Department land remains undisturbed and contains the only known relic, a boundary stone in the cemetery wall. This part of the site is accessible.

The Mobile Battery NZ 514:347

In 1915, following the Bombardment, two mobile 4.7-in guns were placed at Spion Kop, south of the old Cemetery Battery site. Concrete emplacements and a BCP were later added but details are sparse. It is thought that a searchlight may also have been added. The site was closed after the war and the emplacements removed in the 1950s. The site is open but nothing remains.

Fairy Cove Battery* NZ 527:343

Fairy Cove takes its name from a number of old pits which at one time were thought to be Iron Age defensive structures. Also known as Garrisons Point, it had long been the site of artillery and Fairy Cove Battery was built close to the site of the Napoleonic North Battery. This stood on unstable land which had since fallen into the sea and the new battery was built further back alongside the road on land gifted to the War Office by Hartlepool Corporation in 1860. Just across the road a barracks was built for the Militia.

The plot was small, with only room for three emplacements and a side arm store, but as it was close to the barracks this caused few problems. The emplacements comprised two barbettes with a traverse in between. The problem of erosion was not properly addressed at the time of building and the guns were dismounted in 1867 as the emplacements were being undermined. However, the site was of sufficient importance, given its ability to protect the northern approaches, that it was considered in a number of later reports:

A battery for 1-9.2-in. RBL gun and two medium rifled guns should be constructed near the site of Fairy Cove to prevent an enemy's vessel from lying in the waters to the north, from whence could be partially enfiladed the guns in the Heugh Battery. The medium guns should be mounted to sweep the shore along the north sands, where facilities for landing exist.

The site remained in War Department hands and was used as a Volunteer practice battery. One gunner related that mortar balls were collected in wicker baskets at low tide so they could be fired again.

By 1895 the promenade had been extended past Fairy Cove and a new site was built into the structure, but no guns were mounted. In 1904 a DRF post was built for the Cemetery and Heugh Batteries alongside a married quarters for two families. The rangefinder and telephones were mounted on the first floor and the ground floor was fitted out as a washroom. In the years before the war it was also used as the fortress commander's post. However, the situation was far from ideal, particularly when the Cemetery Battery closed in 1907. Lieutenant Colonel Robson began lobbying Northern Command to move the post into the Heugh Battery, finally succeeding in autumn 1914, just before the Bombardment. A new position finder was then mounted in Fairy Cove for practice purposes and used until November 1929 when it was moved into the Lighthouse Battery. The site then fell into disuse and for a time an early breech loading field gun, captured in the First World War, was displayed here.

The buildings were removed but the general shape can be readily discerned as the foundations, built into the promenade, have remained unaltered. As part of the promenade and Town Moor the site is always accessible.

Heugh Battery 1860-1956 *** NZ 531:339

Hartlepool Corporation leased the site of the Heugh Battery to the War Department on 7 December 1859 at a peppercorn rent for 999 years. Work commenced at the Lighthouse and Heugh Batteries on 19 December 1859, to be completed by 28 November 1860 at a total cost of £3,298. Extensive work was required to shore up the crumbling cliffs and caves which riddled the northern part of the site were hand packed with rubble and the entrances bricked up.

Four 68pr guns were installed, three in embrasures with gun No. 4 in a barbette. Two small parade level magazines were provided. The battery buildings were built close together at the northern end of the battery, with the main building containing the master gunner's residence, guard rooms, and stores. All were constructed in brick with flat roofs to keep them below the level of the earth embankment which enclosed the north end. The site was enclosed by a low wooden fence and no attempt was made to provide for close quarter defence.

The 68pr guns were replaced with three 64pr RML of 71cwt (converted from the 8-in shell gun) around 1882. Emplacement No. 3 was filled with a mound of earth to break the line of the battery and give added protection to the remaining guns. Each of the magazines held eighty-eight cartridges in metal-lined cases, giving a capacity of fifty-eight rounds per gun. As the shells could not be stored out in the open, as with the old balls, shell recesses were built into the retaining wall and covered by wooden doors.

In 1888, when the Royal Artillery and Royal Engineers Committee visited the battery, they wrote:

The Committee do not recommend that much money should be spent in improving Heugh Battery. They therefore content themselves with recommending that the platforms should be blocked up and the sills of the embrasures raised. (Royal Artillery and Royal Engineers Works Committee Report No. 82, Minute 800, 1888, PRO WO 396/4)

In 1899 the battery was completely remodelled for two 6-in BL guns, the contract being placed on 21 March 1899 and work commencing on 14 April. The reconstruction took just over a year to complete, being finished on 11 September 1900 at a cost of £4,095. Apart from three small buildings and a walled section containing an old magazine, the original battery was completely demolished. The original gun line was pivoted at an angle to the rear and the ground in front of the guns contoured with a 3 foot 6 inch pad of sand covered with 6 inches of soil to protect against incoming shellfire. Two standard emplacements were built for the Mk VII guns, gun No. 1 (which can be seen today) being a narrow angle and No. 2 a wide angle type. A high brick perimeter wall, with an embrasure for a machine gun, replaced the original fence and new battery buildings, including a small barrack block, were erected to the south of the site.

The magazine complex comprised the usual shell and cartridge stores separated by a small shifting lobby. Two further rooms completed the underground facilities, an RA store and small lamp room. Capacities for the shell and cartridge stores were

1,130 and 1,000 respectively, giving each gun a supply of 500 rounds.

A small open DRF post was built into the retaining wall south of gun No. 1 but this was short-lived, being replaced in 1914 by a single-roomed post. Within the post the rangefinder pedestal comprised a column of concrete buried to a depth of 15 feet, giving the DRF Mk II a height of 56 feet above mean sea level. It also contained two small chart tables and a telephone to the PWSS. Although unheated it was fairly comfortable, with panelled walls and wooden floorboards. Access was by a set of wooden steps from the parade onto the roof of the telephone room and then via concrete steps. It remains in good condition and it was here that Lieutenant Colonel Robson, the fortress commander, sat out the Bombardment. Behind, the small brick telephone room contained direct lines to Fairy Cove, the Lighthouse Battery and the PWSS. Unfortunately the lines were mounted on poles and not channelled underground.

No attempt was made to reinforce the battery buildings as the retaining wall was deemed to provide sufficient protection. The barracks contained room for thirteen men and an NCO room for two. It also held a small cook house, bath and ablution room and gaol house. This building partially stands today. Close by were the smiths and fitters shops, a small electric meter house and the RA store. Some of the earlier battery buildings were retained at the north of the site and in the early years were used as offices and stores for the Royal Engineers. Until 1915 there was no electric supply to the battery and all heating and lighting was by coal and gas. The original magazine was equipped with a Howarth ventilator and converted for use as a machine gun shed.

Shortly after the BCP was completed in 1914, the cartridge and shell recesses in the gun emplacements were reworked. The original 2 inch thick deal (wood) doors were replaced with steel doors and the recesses enlarged to hold 20 cartridges or 25 shells each. It would appear that this was a typical modification throughout the region.

In 1913 Lieutenant Colonel Robson made a few minor modifications of his own. In particular he had a 'jagged camouflage screen' of wood planking fixed on the rear perimeter wall, which had the effect of making the site to appear higher than it actually was. He also moved the fire commander's post and PWSS into the battery and a 30 foot high timber tower was erected for the purpose in 1915. The second floor of this tower held the fire commander's post and sleeping quarters. The PWSS was in a small hut at the top of the tower. Gas lighting was used throughout and radiators fitted in various rooms. Speaking tubes and a telephone were fitted for communication.

In June 1918 Mark IV shields were fitted to both guns and a similar shield fitted to the Lighthouse gun. February 1928 saw the Bombardment guns renewed, the originals being temporarily stored on site and two new 6-in Mk VII fitted. The following year the old guns were sent to North Shields Drill Hall for Tynemouth Heavy Brigade and to the Armoury in West Hartlepool for training the Territorials.

The inter-war years saw a significant change with the incorporation of the Heugh and Lighthouse Batteries in preparation for the fortress plotting system. The Lighthouse gun became Heugh H1, Heugh gun No. 1 was removed and the emplacement abandoned while gun No. 2 remained as H2. A 9 foot Barr and Stroud rangefinder was fitted to the roof of the old battery commander's post. The reason gun No. 1 was removed is unclear but it may be that vibration on firing affected the BCP. The old emplacement did not fall totally out of use as it was used at the start of the Second World War to hold a Lewis gun for anti-aircraft defence.

During 1940 the military presence on the Headland increased significantly and most of Moor Terrace, up to and including the Rovers Club, was requisitioned by the military for use as the battery office, billets and a medical centre. The old barrack block was used as a canteen but could only seat fifty men at a time. To ease pressure on the cooks, an outdoor field kitchen was also set up. A shower block and boiler room were added, followed by a brick-built PAD/gas defence centre which covered much of the old parade. In late 1940 through 1941 a large number of temporary buildings were erected behind the battery and on the Town Moor. These included a much larger kitchen and dining room and twelve huts for accommodation. To train the new recruits a miniature (.22) rifle range was also set up. Sand-bagged blast walls and a pair of air raid shelters were also added.

The final upgrade took place in 1942, with the Heugh and Lighthouse Batteries rearmed as a three-gun CD/AA battery. Although the reworking of the old Mk VII No. 1 emplacement was considered, a new emplacement for gun No. 3 was constructed on the Town Moor but the gun was not fitted. The new emplacement

Heugh Battery in 1943, showing the extent of the wartime site.

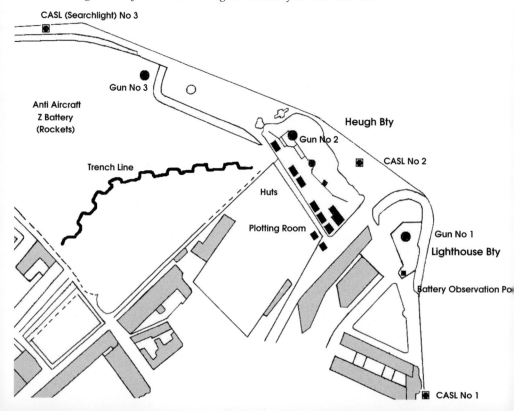

was self-contained with an underground magazine, engine room and shelter. It was intended to upgrade the battery to 5.25-in dual purpose guns but the work was not undertaken. The old Mk VII guns were sent to Dartmouth where they were fitted at Brownstone Battery. Also added was a battery plotting room which linked the new close defence BOP at the Lighthouse and counter-bombardment BOP at Fairy Cove barracks with the Todd Point fire command. The old BCP was by this time redundant and fell into disuse.

The battery went into care and maintenance in 1944, and was reactivated in 1947 until final closure in 1956.

Today there is nothing left to see of the Victorian emplacements as all were demolished or buried as part of the 1900 upgrade. The south magazine with part of the retaining wall still stands, although at the time of writing it is sealed and unexplored. Much of the 1900 concrete remains apart from that affected by the 6-in Mk 24 upgrade. Of particular importance are emplacement No. 1, the BCP and magazines which were used during the Bombardment. The only ancillary building to survive is a section of the barrack block, all the other buildings having been demolished. The battery is currently being restored by the Heugh Gun Battery Trust with the intention of creating a museum. It will be open to the public but the times have yet to be decided.

Lighthouse Battery, 1856-1956 * NZ 531:338

This was the first battery to be activated in the region, although the details are obscure. It appears that the embrasures of the Napoleonic East Battery were rearmed with a number of 32pr smoothbores in 1855 and the site used by the Militia. Construction proper began on 19 December 1859 for two 68pr smoothbore muzzle loaders and the battery was completed almost a year later on 28 November 1860. The new battery was partially built over the old embrasures which were then filled in. It contained two emplacements with a single magazine between, all built of limestone blocks and to the same pattern as the Heugh. gun No. 2, the northern emplacement, was a barbette, to give the widest possible coverage, while No. 1 was an embrasure to cover the harbour entrance only. The plot of land was small, with only enough room in the compound for a small side arm store and all other facilities were sited over the road at the Heugh, a situation which continued throughout the battery's life.

Although well positioned for its purpose, the site had a number of serious drawbacks which were devastating during the Bombardment. The lighthouse gives a perfect aiming mark for enemy guns and housing behind the battery was extremely vulnerable. A large house even stood right next to the gun.

The Subcommittee of 1881 found the battery 'very cramped' and 'it may perhaps be reconstructed for one heavy gun in a shielded casemate', a rare and quite bizarre recommendation for this period. The Inspector General in 1884 concurred 'in the proposed defences at Fairy Cove and Heugh Battery; but consider that a heavy gun at Lighthouse Battery would so greatly add to the security of the bay and entrances to the docks, that it would be advisable to move back the lighthouse in order to gain a site for that purpose.

This appears to be the first acknowledgement of the problems caused by the lighthouse. At the time of the report, the Lighthouse Battery held 'two smooth bore guns, practically obsolete', these being the original 68pr which remained until replaced by 64pr RML between 1882 and 1888. As the new guns were simply slotted in place the Royal Artillery and Royal Engineers Committee could only describe it as 'a slight stone work', but went on to say:

the armourment of Lighthouse Battery should be withdrawn, and that the work should be remodelled to receive 1-6-inch B.L. gun, which would command a wide arc, including the water to the south as well as to the east and north of East Hartlepool. This is the most prominent of the available sites, and a gun mounted here would be comparatively unlikely to draw fire on the docks. It is believed that the removal of the lighthouse, which stands immediately in the rear of the battery, is in contemplation. The lighthouse in this position is most objectionable, and blocks the arc of fire, and, if it is decided to adopt the site for a new gun, every effort should be made to procure its removal. (Report No. 136, Minute 1469, 1894, PRO WO 396/5)

In 1893 it was completely rebuilt as part of the first wave of breech loading HP guns for a single 6-in Mk IV. Two more were placed at Hartlepool, at the Cemetery Battery, the following year. Rebuilding was authorized by the War Office on 30 January 1892 and work commenced on 4 May to be completed by 8 February 1893 at a cost of £2,381. The emplacement was flanked on either side by underground shell and cartridge stores and an open DRF pit and brick telephone room were added. The reconstruction completely erased the old battery. Communication within the battery was by speaking tube and, as the examination battery, a semaphore mast was erected to challenge shipping. A barbed wire entanglement was placed on the northern boundary but the front was left unobstructed, being protected by a 30 foot drop to the shore. To the south a low wall with 4 foot railings was added, while the back of the battery was screened by a 6 foot steel palisade. Despite the later modifications to the emplacement and addition of more buildings, this was to remain the basic layout until 1956.

The Owen Committee recommended upgrading the gun to Mk VII on central pivot mount and authorization for the work was given by Northern Command on 6 April 1908 (although work actually started on 13 January). The conversion was completed on 9 June and cost £418. Further work to increase the storage for ammunition took place between 3 December 1909 and 24 August 1910 at a cost of £55. 15s. 5d. The new emplacement was built into the old by increasing the thickness of the ring wall and constructing a platform within. A few other modifications are noted, in particular the underground shell store was increased in size. The original DRF appears to have been replaced and moved into a new pit

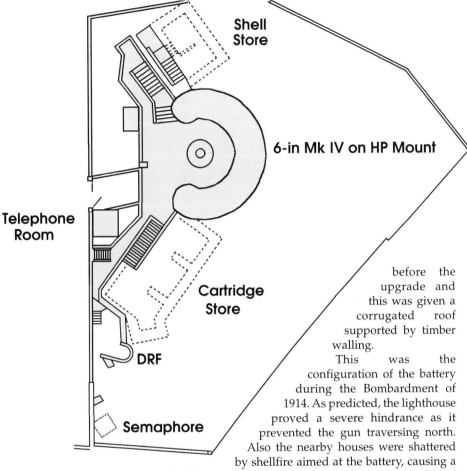

Shell
Store

6-in Mk IV on HP Mount

Telephone
Room

Cartridge
Store

DRF

Semaphore

before the upgrade and this was given a corrugated roof supported by timber walling.

This was the configuration of the battery during the Bombardment of 1914. As predicted, the lighthouse proved a severe hindrance as it prevented the gun traversing north. Also the nearby houses were shattered by shellfire aimed at the battery, causing a number of casualties. The lighthouse was demolished in 1915 and replaced by a temporary timber tower on the Town Moor. Although it was not possible to move the housing, a number of buildings which had been hit were demolished and the ground used to extend the site for a second time. The army had hoped to acquire the land previously occupied by the lighthouse and even designed a large combined DRF/Barr and Stroud rangefinder post for the site. In the event it remained in coastguard hands and a new lighthouse was erected a few yards west of the base of the original.

Between the wars a new BOP for DRF Mk V was added, along with a handful of huts and stores, while a turret was fitted and the gun replaced at the same time as at the Heugh Battery. In 1936 the two batteries were amalgamated, with the Lighthouse gun becoming Heugh Gun H1. The remainder of the batteries' history is considered in the Heugh entry.

When the battery was converted for CD/AA in 1942 the original emplacement was again reworked. This might be unique as no records have yet been found of any other emplacement being upgraded from 6-in Mk IV to 6-in Mk VII to 6-in Mk 24. The battery was demolished in 1967 but there is reason to believe that this amounted to little more than burial. Part of the gun apron can be traced and one building, a shelter from the CD/AA upgrade, remain. The site is on open ground.

Volunteer Practice Batteries at Hartlepool

A Volunteer practice battery was built on the Town Moor around 1860. It was situated thirty yards north of the Heugh Battery, under the later coastguard station and Heugh gun No. 3 site. The small plot held two small buildings and flat platforms for the guns.

The site seems to have been abandoned when the guns were withdrawn from Fairy Cove, which was then used by the Volunteers. Around 1901 a practice battery was in use at West Hartlepool by the Newburn Bridge, where the gunners fired a 64pr RML at a fixed barrel out at sea.

The Examination Battery/Old Pier Battery NZ 526:334

In 1914 at the time of the Bombardment an examination battery was under construction on the Old Pier. It comprised one 4.7-in gun with autosights on the pier and two wide angle searchlights at York Place. A BOP was placed at the end of the pier. The battery was operational between 1915 and 1928-9, when the gun and searchlights were removed.

In 1940 two 12pr 12cwt Mk I guns were placed on the pier for close defence of the harbour, with two 45 degree searchlights again placed at York Place. Manned by regulars from 267 Coast Regiment it went into care and maintenance in November 1943 and was reopened in 1947. The final date of closure is not known.

No remains have been noted, apart from a concrete shelter behind the pier which may have formed part of the battery. The pier and surrounding area are open to the public.

Seaton Carew Battery 1940-5 NZ 522:538

Construction of this emergency battery commenced on 6 April and was completed by 27 July 1940. It was built around the old public swimming baths. The battery contained two 6-in Mk VII guns on Mk III naval central pivot mounts. It remained in service until 11 January 1944, when it was placed on a care and maintenance basis. The site was cleared shortly after this time. The baths, erected in 1914, were used in both world wars as billets by planking over the pool.

The battery was manned by one captain and seven other ranks (315 Coast Regiment) along with eight subalterns and eighty other ranks (Home Guard). One officer and six men made up an offensive patrol.

The site contained a number of facilities which are fairly representative of an emergency battery in 1942: two 6-in Mk VII with magazines and 9 foot Barr and Stroud rangefinder; one 75 mm gun (mobile), one spigot mortar, three AA gun pits; two 90 cm 3 degree (pencil beam) converted AA searchlights under remote control; armed store, office/duty room, sergeants mess, sergeants quarters, training hut, battery HQ, cook house, quiet room, lecture room, gunnery stores, gunnery room, latrine; seven slit trenches and one rifle pit and possibly four pillboxes. The perimeter comprised triple layer danart wire and the surrounding beach was mined. The site is on open ground but nothing remains.

Pasley (Coatham Battery)

See Palliser Battery for general details of this site. After the withdrawal of the Palliser gun in 1928 it was proposed to mount that gun here but the work was not undertaken. The battery was completely camouflaged using hessian and netting during the Second World War and a blast wall was added. It remained in service until November 1943 when it went into care and maintenance before finally closing in 1949, when the gun and mount went to Woolwich. During the war it was manned by 117 Coast Regiment.

The nearby barracks held a 30 foot Barr and Stroud rangefinder atop a 94 foot high lattice tower with the BOP beneath and a second rangefinder was placed in the Coatham Hotel. Both were linked to Todd Point fortress command post which controlled the Hartlepool and Tees defences from the late 1930s onward. Todd Point comprised a fortress plotting room and observation post containing a position finder Mk IIa. The self-contained compound was supplemented in the Second World War with trenches, pillboxes and two spigot mortar pits. It worked in conjunction with a position finder located north of Hartlepool at Blackhall but few details of this have come to light. Todd Point remained in service until 1956.

There were also two concrete emplacements at West Coatham, of which only rubble now remains, but it has not been possible to establish the guns or a date.

The site is not accessible and the battery has been completely demolished or buried.

South Gare Battery and Submarine Mine Depot ** NZ 555:248

Prior to the construction of the North and South Gare breakwaters, the entrance to the Tees was treacherous with shifting channels and no defences were thought necessary. With the growth of Middlesbrough and the completion of the South Gare breakwater in 1887 the recommendations of the Royal Artillery and Works Committee were undertaken and South Gare Battery and a submarine mining depot were built. The land was leased from the Tees Commissioners for sixty-three years and work commenced on 15 October 1890, to be completed by 27 February 1892 at a cost of £8,852.

Two 4.7-in guns covered the mouth of the Tees and another four emplacements were provided as alternate sites to cover either side of the breakwater by a pair of

6pr guns. Two small emplacements for Maxim guns were also provided. Extensive underground facilities were built, as along with the usual magazines and shelters there was a large engine room with coal store and electric control room as well as a test room and passage. In 1903 the old engine house was cleared and oil generators installed and the BCP reconstructed. In 1907 the mining depot closed and the 6pr guns withdrawn, although the depot continued to act as a barracks with stores and workshops for the battery. A new director's post was also built for the searchlights, as was done at other depots which had closed in the area.

In 1914 a PWSS was added and it was this post which first spotted the German battlecruisers on their way to bombard Hartlepool, but unfortunately the enemy vessels were mostly shrouded by fog and due to the general confusion not fired on. By the time their nationality had been established they were too far north and out of sight of the battery.

It was decommissioned in 1920 when Pasley battery opened and the guns were dismounted. They were left on site until 1929 when they were sold for scrap and the remainder of the battery dismantled. The site remained in War Department hands and took part in the 'Whisky War' exercise of 1934 when an 18pr field gun and director were temporarily used to simulate an active battery.

In July 1938 the battery was reactivated with the mounting of two 6-in Mk VII guns on Mk II CP mounts. A new gun No. 1 emplacement of standard wide angle design was built on the east side of the breakwater road to protect the southern side of the breakwater. This emplacement was built on a huge stone-walled foundation on the side of the breakwater and contained a small magazine. Gun No. 2 was built over the old 4.7-in gun A2 and appears to have used the original magazines. Several new buildings were also erected during the upgrade, including a new BOP containing a DRF Mk IIIb, lecture hall, apparatus hut and various stores.

The Second World War saw extensive beach defences added to South Gare, some of which still remain. Just opposite the submarine mine depot are four holdfasts backed up by a concrete trench built into the road wall at 555:280.

The submarine mine depot was built at 555:278, the whole being enclosed by a concrete wall loopholed on three sides. A concrete slipway led from the large boathouse into the small harbour known as 'Paddy's Hole' and the interior was filled with the various stores and accommodation. A second slipway was added later, leading directly into the estuary. A narrow gauge rail line ran the length of the breakwater to the depot to transport the mines. The depot closed in 1907, the site being transferred to the Fortress Engineers, although the boat house was reacquired by the artillery in 1931 when it was used to store towed targets for practice at the Hartlepool batteries. During the Second World War an FW3/23 type pillbox was added, overlooking the south-west corner of the loopholed wall.

In 1953 the lease expired and both battery and the converted mining depot were closed. The battery site was left derelict and is now largely buried and difficult to interpret. Emplacement No. 1 (1938) is largely intact, although the pit has been filled in. Emplacement No. 1 (1892) is similarly filled and only the apron is exposed, while emplacement A2 is breaking up. The mining depot is largely intact, having continued in use by a local boat club and the loopholed wall is probably a unique survivor. Although on private land, the site apart from the mine depot compound is accessible to the public. There are parking places along the length of the breakwater.

Whitby Battery

Two 6-in Mk VII guns on naval PVIII mounts were emplaced in this Home Guard emergency battery on 11 June 1940. The BOP contained a DRF Mk IIb and two 90 cm 3 degree searchlights were provided. The battery was controlled by Tees fire command which could relay radar data via a WS no. 9 set. Later a direct link was made to Goldsborough Radar Station. There are no known remains of this site.

Wheatcroft/Scarborough Battery

Two 6-in Mk XII guns were mounted on naval P.VII* mounts on 14 June 1940 for this emergency battery manned by the Home Guard. The BOP contained a DRF Mk IIb and two 90 cm 3 degree searchlights were provided. The guns were controlled by Tees fortress command which could relay radar data via a WS no. 9 set. The site has been levelled, with only buried earthworks remaining.

Filey Battery

The two 6-in Mk XI* guns dating from 1910 were fitted on naval P.V mounts on 15 June 1940. It is recorded that the southern gun, originally from HMS *Lion* was manned by Home Guard and the northern gun by 320 Bty RA. A generator room for the searchlights was located between the guns, with the BOP containing a DRF Mk IIb above. The 90 cm 3 degree searchlights were emplaced on the lower cliff. The guns were controlled by Tees fortress command which could relay radar data via a WS no. 9 set. Later data could be received directly from Bempton Radar station The site has been levelled and is falling into the sea but some traces are still visible on the ground.

HUMBER DEFENCES

A commercial port of considerable importance, liable to cruiser raid. (Montgomery, 1899)

Ringborough/Aldbrough Battery TA 273:372

A purpose-built three 6-in Mk 24 high angle gun battery erected 1942-3. A farm was occupied to provide offices and other facilities and a barracks constructed 150 yards to the north. Three emplacements spaced 75 yards apart were laid out in a line just in front of the farm, with small magazines 100-200 feet behind each. All

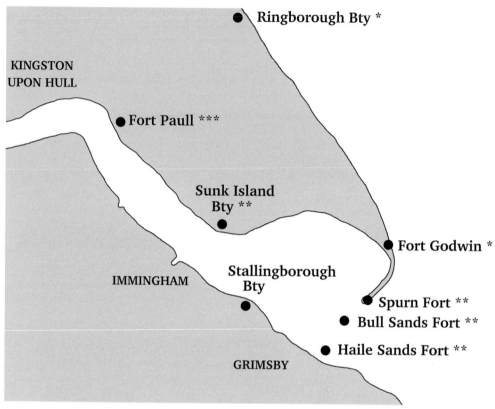

Humber defences.

were connected by concrete-lined trenches. A brick BOP was erected in the farm complex, with another to the north for radar and one to the south for the two CASL. The guns were fitted on Mk V mountings.

On private land: there are some remnants, including the BOP and magazines. However, the site is now falling into the sea.

Fort Godwin / Kilnsea Battery ** TA 418:160

Construction began in 1915 for a twin 9.2-in Mk X gun battery with two magazines built of concrete. The battery buildings were built in a line, behind the emplacements, protected by a slight rise in the land. The BC post stood to the north and this was connected by tunnel to a shelter 100 yards to the west. Another tunnel led from in front of the guns to a blockhouse built onto the sea wall that protected the site. Between the battery and the Blue Bell Inn extensive barracks and officers mess and quarters were built. An anti-aircraft battery was also built here during the First World War, with a searchlight station and AA height finder located just to

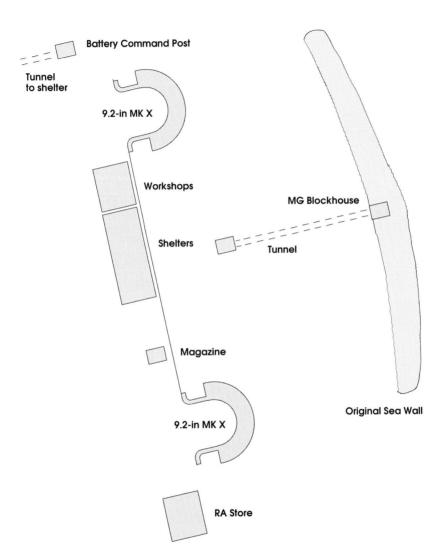

Fort Godwin, Kilnsea battery.

Workshops and shelters at Fort Godwin.

the north of the battery, along with a sound mirror. The battery was decommissioned after the war but reactivated as a 3.7-in anti-aircraft battery during the Second World War and many of the buildings on the present campsite behind probably date from this time.

The gun line has recently fallen over the crumbling cliff and the shelters and workshops will follow soon. The broken emplacements and magazines now lie on the beach and are slowly sinking. The site is a caravan and holiday park with easy access. Slightly north, in a private field, the sound locator can still be seen. This has

A huge concrete bowl stranded on the beach: the remnants of a 9.2-in emplacement at Fort Godwin.

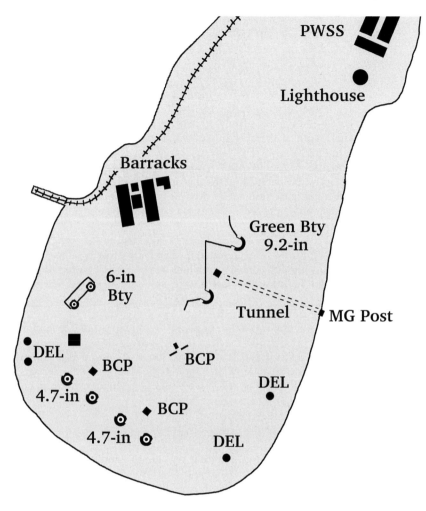

Spurn Head.

been given protected status.

Spurn Fort TA 399:106 **

During the muzzle loading years Spurn Head was often considered but the main setback was that any guns mounted there would not have sufficient range to close the estuary to enemy shipping. The introduction of the breech loader partially resolved the problem but only a small number of 4.7-in and 6-in guns were mounted. At the start of the First World War significant work was undertaken to close the estuary. Green Battery was built on Spurn Head supplemented by a similar battery at Kilnsea and the seaforts of Haile and Bull Sand which are described below. Also on Spurn Head were two batteries of 4.7-in guns at the extreme tip, with their own defence electric lights and observation posts and a twin 6-in battery which appears to have mounted a practice 4-in gun later. By 1922 all the guns had either been withdrawn or marked down for practice only, except for the 4.7-in guns. Barracks were built which still stand as part of the coastguard complex. To ease building and supply, a narrow gauge military railway was laid down along the length of the spit, fragments of which, including the turntable foundations, can still be seen. The railway was unusual as among the carriages which could traverse it were two 'sail trucks' propelled by a lug sail suspended from a 14 foot mast and capable of reaching 40 miles per hour. These trucks had no brakes and were apparently stopped by dropping a heavy piece of timber in front of the wheels. Presumably the sails were furled first and this was only done at low speed.

During the First World War a large concrete and steel tower was built as the PWSS just north of Spurn Head Lighthouse, alongside other military buildings. Little now remains, although some foundations can be traced. During the Second World War two of the 4.7-in emplacements were converted to mount 6-in guns and recommendations were made for upgrading to 5.25-in CD/AA but the work was not carried out.

Many structures still remain but are gradually being buried under sand dunes. Indeed in 1922 it was noted that the searchlights were of little use as they were silting up even then. Spurn Head is a conservation area and open to the public, though the visitor should be aware that, although the road is suitable for cars, it is closed to the public, with parking at Kilnsea where refreshments can also be had. It is nevertheless a pleasant walk to the batteries.

Green Battery TA 398:106 **

A First World War 9.2-in battery mounting two guns, standing on Spurn Head, built in 1915. As with Kilnsea Battery a tunnel ran from in front of the guns to a machine gun emplacement on the coast line. By 1919 the 9.2-in guns were used for practice only and were withdrawn shortly afterward.

During the Second World War the 9.2-in emplacements were converted for anti-aircraft guns.

Sunk Island Battery ** TA 2496:1756

Rebuilt in the First World War, Sunk Island Battery was one of three intended to replace Paull Point by moving the defences closer to the mouth of the Humber. Work for two 6-in Mk VII was completed in 1915 and comprised the two emplacements with magazine between, smiths and fitters shops, a small barracks block and warrant officers quarters all contained in a roughly hexagon-shaped compound. At the end of the war the guns were withdrawn.

The battery was reactivated during the Second World War when two 4.7-in guns were mounted in the old emplacements. It was then finally closed in 1943.

The remains are now in poor condition, the BOP is partially demolished and the CASL are gone.

Fort Paull *** TA 169 225

Her Majesty's steamer *Cuckoo*, Commander Brockman RN, arrived here on Tuesday, from Sheerness, having been placed at the services of a committee appointed by the Government to inspect the river Humber and decide on the most eligible site for the erection of a fort, the Present Citadel being useless as a place of defence. The committee consists of Colonel Brereton RN conservator of the Humber, Mr Dale Brown, Commodore of pilots and E K Calver, admiralty surveyor. It is believed that a new fort will be erected at Paull or in the immediate *neighbourhood.'* (The Fort Paull Story (visitor guide) (*Fort Paull Heritage Organisation, 2001*))

Fort Paull.

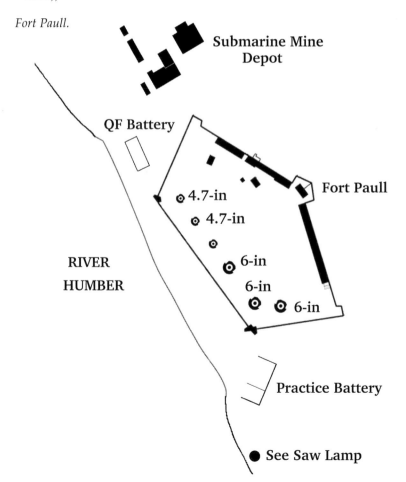

Fort Paull, also known as Point Battery, was built between 1861 and 1863 to replace the Citadel, an obsolete fortification on the riverbank at Hull, dating to 1681. The Citadel with its thirteen guns survived as headquarters for the Hull Volunteer Artillery until 1863 when it was demolished. Paull Fort is believed to have been built over a Napoleonic fort, itself built on the site of the Civil War Paull Cliff Battery, but this has not been verified as no remains have been found of the earlier works. The site is down river from Hull and was chosen to close the channel before the town. It has a roughly pentagonal outline formed by an embankment and dry ditch and is the only example of a Victorian fort in the north of England. Also unique are two caponiers comprising two bombproof tunnels leading from the embankment corners to two-storey blockhouses overlooking the Humber. The original muzzle loading battery mounted nineteen 68pr facing south and west, mounted in brick embrasures, which were replaced with 64pr RML some time before 1871 when two spare guns were also placed on standing carriages at High Paull House for ornamental purposes until being issued to the Hull Volunteers in 1876. The house was often in use.

Significant upgrading began in 1894 when the old emplacements were demolished to make way for three 6-in Mk VI on HP mounts and two 4.7-in guns with magazines built into and under the embankment. In 1904, when the 6-in guns were upgraded to Mk VII, it appears that one of the emplacements (No. 3) was abandoned and a new one constructed. The site was visited by Owen in 1905 who declared the 4.7-in guns redundant, although Dalton in 1907 argued that they should be kept as one was the examination gun and both were useful to the Volunteers. Three electric lights were emplaced on the banks of the river and an engine room constructed within the battery in 1907 and a director's post doubling as a battery commander's post in the empty emplacement added in 1912. By the First World War, following the completion of batteries at Sunk Island and Stallingborough, the battery became superfluous and the 6-in guns were removed in 1915, although the site continued in service as HQ Humber Fire Command. During the 1920s two 6-in guns were remounted and used by the Territorials as a practice battery until their removal before the Second World War. The fort continued as the fire command for the duration of the war and a new observation post was added, while the remainder of the site was used as a store for anti-aircraft ammunition and home to a degaussing station, staffed by WRENS, to demagnetize outgoing vessels to safeguard them against mines. The old director's post was pressed into service as the monitoring post, while the ammunition storage entailed some changes to the barracks and officers quarters in order to strengthen them. The fort remained in use until 1956 and was sold on into private ownership in 1961.

In 1886 a submarine mining establishment was established just north of the fort, which entailed the construction of a jetty fitted and rail line running to the depot. Officers quarters and a barracks block were also built and High Paull House was put into use as a classroom. The mining observation post and a test range were constructed within the fort itself. The depot completed in June 1886 cost £5,409 and the jetty was completed in the November at a cost of £4,877. Between 1895 and 1905 an unusual 'see-saw' searchlight was built to the south of the fort for the mining

This 7-in Armstrong RML is now on display at Fort Paull.

depot. This was unearthed in 2002 and then reburied to preserve it for future archaeologists.

Also associated with Fort Paull were two Volunteer practice batteries, the first of which was erected in 1860 next to Earles shipyard and equipped with four 32pr smoothbores. It was abandoned in 1884 to make way for the new Alexandra Dock and a new site just to the east of Fort Paull was selected for four 64pr RML, two of which were emplaced and mounted on slides in 1887. They were replaced by two 3pr quick fire guns in 1905.

The fort remains in very good condition and has been preserved as a private museum. Surprisingly, there is access throughout, including all the magazines and caponiers which are well lit and as with the rest of the site packed with a huge range of artefacts and tableaux, ranging from coast defence to replica Crown Jewels and the fort ghost. Above ground are a miscellany of fighting vehicles and guns, some of which are mounted in the emplacements as described below.

No. 1: 4.7-in emplacement currently mounting 3.7-in AA gun
No. 2: 4.7-in emplacement currently mounting 12pr QF
No. 3: 6-in Mk VI HP emplacement with DEL director's observation post
No. 4: 6-in Mk VI HP emplacement converted for Mk VII, empty
No. 5: 6-in Mk VI HP emplacement converted for Mk VII mounting Armstrong 7-in RML
No. 6: 6-in Mk VII emplacement mounting 3.7-in AA gun

It is open throughout the year and ideal for a family visit, with food and drink on site. A small shop sells a guide, postcards and assorted items with a military theme.

A building associated with the submarine mining establishment stands at 1702:2576.

Bull Sands Fort ** TA 370:093

In June 1914 two admirals and three generals representing the Home Forts Defence Committee visited the Humber and concluded that two sea forts should be built to protect the mouth of the river. Their guns were intended to engage any vessel attempting to enter the estuary, particularly U-boats which would be forced to the surface by booms strung between the two forts. Sea forts were chosen because it was feared that enemy vessels could sneak into the estuary under cover of fog unseen by the shore batteries. Construction at Bull Sand began in 1915 and finished in 1919, resulting in a four-storey hexagonal sea fort mounting two 4-in Mk V guns on 20 degree mounts and two 6pr guns.

The concrete and masonry structure with 12 inch thick steel armour was difficult to build, as the foundations of interlocking steel piles stood on a sandbank 11 feet below low water. Construction cost over one million pounds. Its guns worked in conjunction with Haile Sand Fort and an anti-submarine boom, in the form of a net suspended from a heavy chain, was operated between the two. The fort stood 50 feet above high water and contained three storeys and a basement protected by 12 inch thick steel plate armour. It was capable of accommodating 200 officers and men along with the equipment and provisions required for an extended stay.

The 4-in QF Mk V was brand new, having been introduced in 1915. It had a semi-automatic breech mechanism and used brass cartridges giving a high rate of fire. The whole was protected by a large shield and they are thought to be the only naval guns of this mark to be adopted for coast defence. It was declared obsolete in 1928 when the guns were removed, to be replaced by 6-in guns during the Second World War.

Bull Sand Fort is reputed to have been the site of the first casualty in mainland Britain during the Second World War when a Lewis gunner opened fire on a German mine-laying aircraft which then returned fire. The gunner was wounded in the leg by a ricochet.

The fort stands today but can only be reached by boat. A number of proposals have been put forward for its future use, including a drug rehabilitation centre, but at present it stands empty. Due to the difficulty of reaching Bull Sand and Haile Sand Forts they are the least disturbed and most complete examples of coast defences in the region. It goes without saying that these sites are not accessible to the public.

Haile Sand Fort ** TA 349:062

Haile Sand is slightly smaller than its sister, Bull Sand Fort, and mounted two 4-in Mk V and two 6pr guns. It can be reached by foot at low tide but be (seriously) warned: the tide comes in very quickly. There is no public access.

BIBLIOGRAPHY

COAST DEFENCE

English Heritage, *Twentieth Century Military Sites* (English Heritage, 2000).

Hogg, I V, *Coast Defences of England and Wales 1856-1956* (David & Charles, 1974).

Jones, K W Maurice, *History of Coast Defence in the British Army* (Royal Artillery Institution, 1959).

Lowry, B (ed.), *Twentieth Century Defences in Britain: An Introductory Guide* (Council of British Archaeology, 1996).

Moore, D, *Arming the Forts* (Palmerston Forts Society, 1994).

Moore, D, *A Handbook of Military Terms* (Palmerston Forts Society, 1996).

Stevenson, I, *Fort Logs* (Palmerston Forts Society, 2000).

Stevenson, I, *The Redan No 5, Tees and Hartlepool Defences* (Palmerston Forts Society, Feb. 2001).

HARTLEPOOL AND THE 1914 BOMBARDMENT

[Anon.], *The German Raid on the Hartlepools* (Sage Bookseller & Stationer, 1915).

Bailey, B, 'The Artillery Defence of Hartlepool', *Journal of Royal Artillery*, CII (1975).

Bullen, J, The German Battlecruiser Attack on the East Coast Ports (*Imperial War Museum*, date).

Marsay, M, *Bombardment: The Day the East Coast Bled* (Great Northern Publishing, 1999).

Miller, F, *Under Shell Fire: The Hartlepools Scarborough and Whitby under German Shell Fire* (Robert Martin Ltd, 1915).

Miller, F, The Hartlepools in the Great War (Sage Bookseller & Stationer, 1920).

Murley, W A, 'The Bombardment of the Hartlepools', *Journal of Royal Artillery*, LXI (1934).

Robson, L, 'Bombardment of Hartlepools', *Journal of Royal Artillery*, XLVIII (1921).

Ward, J M, *Dawn Raid* (Atkinson Print, 1989).

Yorke, F A, 'The Bombardment of Hartlepool', *Journal of the Royal Artillery*, LVII (1930)

MILITIA AND VOLUNTEERS

Litchfield, N H, *The Militia Artillery 1852-1909* (Sherwood Press, 1987).

Litchfield, N, and Westlake, R, *The Volunteer Artillery 1859-1908: Their Lineage, Uniforms and Badges* (Sherwood Press, 1982).

Saunders, R, *History of the 2nd East Riding RGA Volunteers Hull* (Walker & Brown, 1907).

Westlake, R A, *Royal Engineers: Volunteers 1859-1908* (Sherwood Press, 1983).

TECHNOLOGY

Brown, D K, *From Warrior to Dreadnought* (Chatham, 1997).

Campbell, D, *War Plan UK* (Paladin, 1982).

Hogg, I, *Allied Artillery of World War One* (Crowood Press, 1998).

Hogg, I, *Allied Artillery of World War Two* (Crowood Press, 1999).

Latham, C, and Stobbs, A, *Radar: A Wartime Miracle* (Sutton Publishing Ltd, 1996).

Smith, R D (ed.), *British Naval Armaments, Royal Armories Conference* Proceedings (Dorset Press, 1989).

Wilkinson-Latham, R J, *Discovering Artillery* (Shire Publications, 1972).

GENERAL PUBLICATIONS

Beckett, I, *The Victorians at War* (Hambledon and London, 2003).

Bilton, P, *The Home Front in the Great War* (Pen and Sword, 2003).

Churchill, W, *The Second World War*, vol. 2, *Their Finest Hour* (Cassell & Co, 1949).

Encyclopaedia Britannica (1911).

Hill, R, *War at Sea in the Ironclad Age* (Cassell, 2000).

Ireland, B, *War at Sea 1914-45* (Cassell, 2002).

Kieser, E, *Operation Sealion* (Cassell Military Paperbacks, 1997).

Knight, S M, *The History of the Great European War*, vol. 3 (Caxton, date).

Lipson, E, *Europe in the Nineteenth Century* (Adam and Charles Black, 1955).

Mcleod, R, and Kelly, D, *The Ironside Diaries 1937-40* (Constable, date)

Massie, R K, *Castles of Steel* (Jonathan Cape, 2004).

Wilson, H W (ed.), *The Great War: The Standard History of the All Europe Conflict*, vol. 3 (Amalgamated Press, 1915).

LOCAL PUBLICATIONS

'Hartlepool Charter Celebrations Brochure' (Hartlepool Borough Council, 1951).

Martin, R, *Historical Notes and Personal Reflections of West Hartlepool and its Founder* (1924).

Richmond, T, *Local Records of Stockton and the Neighbourhood*.

Ward, J M, *A Hartlepool Chronology* (Atkinson Print, 2000).

SOURCE MATERIAL

Public Records Office
WO27: War Office inspection returns
WO33: War Office reports and memoranda
WO78: War Office maps and plans
WO192: Fort Record Books
WO199: Military HQ papers, Home Forces.
WO396/4: Royal Artillery and Royal Engineers Works Committee Report No 82, Minute 800, 1888.
WO396/5: Royal Artillery and Royal Engineers Works Committee Report No 136, Minute 1469, 1894.

Durham County Records Office
D/DLI6/1/6-7 Durham RHA Scrapbooks 1856-1938 and 1938 to 1956.

Unpublished papers
Davidson, J (o'Heugh), Hartlepools Association With The Royal Regiment of Artillery, undated typescript.
Roberts, S, Lecture on Bombardment, 1976.

INDEX

12-in BL gun, 58, 72, 134-5
12pr QF gun, 51-3, 72
32pr smooth bore, 45
3.7-in AA gun, 58, 63
4.7-in BL gun, 53-4, 72
4-in QF gun, 58, 72, 167
5.25-in CD/AA gun, 56-7, 72, 141
64pr RML, 47-8
68pr smooth bore, 46-7
6-in gun, various marks, 54-7
6pr QF gun, 51, 58
6pr twin gun, 53
7.5-in BL gun, 58, 140
7-in 110pr gun, 43
9.2-in gun, various marks, 58
Abb's Point Battery, 21, 141
Accidents, 84, 101
Admiralty Intelligence, Room 40, 30, 97-8, 118
Aldbrough (Ringborough) Battery, 157-58
Alexandria, 1882 bombardment, 15
Anti-aircraft guns, see also CD/AA, 32-3, 36
Arbuthnot, Major General, 24
ARP, 36
Artillery Volunteers, 13, 20
Aube, Theophile, Rear Admiral, French Minister of Marine, 28
Autosights, 64

Ballard, George, Commodore First Class, Admiral of Patrols, 102
Balloons, 78
Barbette emplacement, 43
Barr and Stroud rangefinder, 62

Barrons Battery, 142
Battery command post, 25, 61
Battery observation post, 67, 69
Battery plotting rooms, 66
Beach batteries, 38
Beatty, David, Admiral, 98, 116
Bempton Radar Station, 68, 157
Blue Water school, 30
Blyth Battery, 133-34
Blyth, 'landing' in 1913 exercise, 30
Boer War, 27, 77
Bolt from the Blue school, 30
Boundary stones, 42
Breech loading guns, 18, 48-50
Brook, Alan, General, C in C Home Forces, 38
Bull Sand Fort, 31, 166
Burgoyne, John Fox, Inspector General of Fortifications, 9, 10, 11

Callaghan, George, C in C Home Fleet, 30
Camps, 35, 41, 85-6
Cardwell, Edward, Secretary of State for War, 13, 14
Cargo Fleet, proposed fort, 11
Case I-III, laying of guns, 64-5
Cavendish, Spencer, Secretary of State for War, 16
CD/AA, see Coast Defence Anti Aircraft Batteries
Cemetery Battery, 21, 83, 101, 112, 145-6
Chain Home Low Coast Defence stations, 39, 68
Cherburg Naval Base, 10

Childrens Friend, 111, 118
Churchill, Winston, 31, 37, 39, 68, 116
Clarke, Andrew, Inspector General of Fortifications, 15
Cliffords Fort, 19, 17, 21, 73, 139-40
Close Defence, 36
Coastal Crust, 38
Coastal Patrol Organization, 29-30, 102, 104, 125, 128
Coast Artillery Searchlights, 70
Coast Brigade, 11, 20-1, 73
Coast Defence Anti Aircraft Batteries, 39-42, 50, 56-7
Coastguard, 22, 29
Coatham Battery, 155
Committee of Imperial Defence, 96
Competitions, 81-3, 87
Counter bombardment, 32, 36, 40, 50
Crimean War, 10

Dalton, Jason, Major General, 27
Dardanelles, 31-2
Defence Electric Lights, 69
Depression Rangefinder, 59-62
Devon Battery, 140
Directors posts, 70-1
Disbandment of coast defence, 42
District Establishment, 35, 73
Dogger Bank, 125
Dogs, 91-2, 108
DRF, see Depression Rangefinder
Drill years, 35
Druridge Battery, 133
Durham and Edinburgh RGA, 77
Durham Artillery Militia Corps, 9, 77
Durham Fortress Engineers, 27
Durham Light Infantry, 18bn PALS, 102-3, 107, 130

Durham RGA, 24, 33, 101, 124, 130, 140

East and North Yorkshire Artillery Militia Corps, 9
East Riding of Yorkshire RGA, 24, 27
Elbe, German Fisheries Gunboat, 88-9
Elswick Works, 16-17, 46, 54, 132
Embrasure emplacement, 43
Emergency batteries, 39, 56
Emplacement design, 43-4, 55-6
Engine rooms, 69
Examination service, 22-3
Expeditionary force, 27

Fairy Cove Battery, 11, 16, 146-7
Filey Battery, 157
Filey, 'Invasion force', 30
Fire command post, 32
Fisher, John Arbuthnot 'Jackie', First Sea Lord, 28, 97
Five Power Naval Treaty of 1922, 33-4
Fort Coulson, 133
Fort Godwin. 158-60
Fort Paull (Paull Point Battery) 11, 15, 21, 25-6, 31, 69-71, 73, 84, 163-6
Fort Paull, Submarine Mine Depot, 19
Fort Prospect, battle, 77
Fortress command, 29, 36
Fortress plotting system, 36, 66-8
Frenchmans Point Battery (fort), 21, 31, 40, 58

Gallipoli 31-2
GHQ Line, 38
Gloucester Battery, 134
Goldsborough Radar Station, 68, 157

Great Yarmouth, bombardments, 96, 129

Green Battery, 32, 162

Grimsby, 16

Hague Convention, 97

Haile Sand Fort, 31, 167

Haldane, Richard, Secretary of State for War, 27

Hartlepool, bombardment of, 95-129

Hartley Tyne Turret, 134-5

Hart Warren Battery, 143-5

Heavy Brigades, 85-9

Heligoland Bight, 96, 116

Heugh Battery, 11, 16, 21, 31, 56, 73, 85, 88-93, 100, 103, 106-12, 124, 148-51

Heugh Gun Battery Trust, 151

High Seas Fleet, 96-100, 129

Hipper, Admiral, 97-9, 105, 116-17

HMS *Doon*, 102, 104-5, 116, 130

HMS *Dreadnought*, 29

HMS *Dryad*, 24

HMS *Forward*, 102, 112

HMS *Halcyon*, 96

HMS *Illustrious*, 135

HMS *Moy*, 102, 105

HMS *Patrol*, 102, 112, 130

HMS *Test*, 102, 105

HMS *Thunderer*, 14

HMS *Warrior*, 10, 14, 43

HMS *Waveney*, 102

Holy Island Volunteer Practice Battery, 133

Home Guard (see also LDV), 37, 40

Horsley, John, 111, 118

Hull Artillery Volunteers, 19, 59, 79-80

Humber Defences, of 1888, 21, of 1914, 31

Humphrey, Colonel, Hull Volunteers, scandal, 79-81

Hydro pneumatic guns, 18, 21-2, 48-50, 54

Imperial Service List, 28

Inchkieth, 35

Infra red sighting experiments, 137

Ingenohl, Friedrich von, Admiral, C in C High Seas Fleet, 96-9

Invasion preparations of 1940, 37

Ironside, Edmund, General, C in C Home Forces, 37

Jellicoe, John, Admiral, 96

Jeune École, 28

Joint Naval and Military Commission, 20

Jones, Theo, Private DLI, 103, 107

Jutland, 129

Kagoshima, bombardment, 43

Kiel Canal, 29

Kilnsea Battery, 32, 158-60

Kilnsea Sound Mirror, 160

Kings Cup, 87

Kinley Hill Radar Station, 68

Kitchener Battery, 136

Krupp BL gun, 14

La Gloire, 10

LDV (see also Home Guard), 37

Lighthouse Battery, 11, 16, 21, 31, 36, 56, 88, 100, 103-10, 112, 115, 122, 151-4

Link House Battery, 133

Long Scar Rocks, proposed battery of 1883, 16

Magazine lamps, 44

Magazines, 44, 49-50

Marsden Tyne Turret, 136
May, Sir William, Admiral of the
    Fleet, 30
Militia, 17, 74-8
Militia Act of 1852, 9
Moncrief, Colin Scott, 15, 49
Montgomery Report, 132, 143, 145,
    157
Morley Commission of 1883, 15
Munich Crisis, 36, 89

Napier, Charles, 9
Napoleonic batteries, 8, 43, 136
Napoleon III,10
National Artillery Association, 13,
    81
National Servicemen, 41
Northern Command Ladies Cup, 87
Northern Division, Militia Artillery,
    17
North Foreland, 35
Northumberland Artillery Militia,
    9, 13
Northumberland RGA, 24

Old Bess, Tynemouth 9.2-in gun, 35,
    58, 137
Old Pier (Examination) Battery, 100,
    154
Operation Sealion, 37
Orsini, Felice, 10
Owen Report of 1905, 26, 152

Palliser Battery, 32, 50, 143-5
Palliser method, 46
Palmerston Follies, 10
Palmerston Forts, 10
Palmerston, Henry John Temple,
    Home Secretary, Prime Minister,
    10
Park Battery, 39, 50, 57, 140-1

Pasley Battery, 32, 50, 88, 155
Paull Point Battery, see Fort Paull
Pile, Frederick, General, 39
Pillboxes, 37-8, 51
Port War Signal Station, 23, 29
Position Finder, 59-60
Practice Batteries, 45, 133, 154

Quick Fire gun, 17, 48, 51

Radar stations, 39, 68
Radio direction finding stations,
    30
Rangefinding, 59-68
Ravenscar Radar Station, 68
Repository, 11, 83
Rifled muzzle loading guns, 14, 45-8
Ringborough Battery, 157-8
Roberts Battery, 134-5
Robson, Lancelot, Lt Colonel, 85,
    100-4, 107-9, 113, 124-8, 149
Roker Battery, 141
Room 40, Admiralty Intelligence,
    30, 97-8, 118
Rotor Programme, 41-2
Royal Artillery and Royal
    Engineers Works Committees, 19,
    21, 148, 151-2
Royal Artillery Invalids, 11
Royal Commission, 10
Royal Engineers, 18, 43, 130
Royal Field Artillery, 24, 27
Royal Garrison Artillery, 24, 35, 85
Royal Horse Artillery, 24
Royal Marines, 39

Saltburn Radar Station, 68
Scapa Flow, 33, 96-7, 125
Scarborough Battery, 157
Scarborough, bombardment, 97,
    116-17, 129

Scarborough Castle and Militia Depot, 11, 6
Scotch up, 11
Seaham, Batteries, 21, 141-2
Seaham, shelling of, 129
Searchlights, 17, 68-70
Seaton Battery (Blyth), 133
Seaton Carew Battery, 39, 154
Seaton Carew, proposed batteries of 1883, 16
Siege batteries, 33, 124
Singapore, fortifications, 34, 66
Slade, Fred, Major General, 24
Smooth bore guns, 46-7
SMS *Blucher*, 98-9, 107-9, 112, 125
SMS *Derfflinger*, 98, 116
SMS *Kolburg*, 116
SMS *Moltke*, 98-100, 111-12, 125
SMS *Seydlitz*, 98-100, 109-13, 125
SMS *Von der Tann*, 98-9, 116
SMS *Yorck*, 96
South Gare Battery, 21, 31, 50-1, 83, 88, 100, 105-6, 155-7
South Gare, Submarine Mine Depot, 19, 155-7
Spanish Battery, 17, 21, 31, 51, 137-9
Special Reserve Royal Field Artillery, 27
Spion Kop, Mobile Battery, 146
Spurn Head, 15, 31-2, 161-2
Stallingborough Battery, 15
Stanhope, Edward, Secretary of State for War, 19
Stockill, Len, Bdr, 89-93
Submarine *C9*, 102, 112
Submarine *D5*, 96
Submarine Miners, 18-20, 27, 81
Sunderland, 'landing' in 1913 exercise, 30
Sunk Island Battery, 162-3

Tees Defences, in 1888, 21, in 1914, 31
Territorial Army, 35, 39, 41
Territorial Force, 27, 35
Tirpitz, German Minister of Defence, 28-9
Todd Point Fortress Command Post 88, 151, 155
Torpedo boats, 17
Trenchmann, Oscar, Heugh Battery Commander, 103, 106-7, 109-13, 124, 126
Trenchmann, Richard 'Dickie', Lighthouse Battery Commander, 103, 107-10, 115
Trow Point, 141
Tyne Coast Defence Command, 24
Tyne Defences, in 1888, 21, in 1914, 31
Tynemouth Castle, 11, 17, 21, 31, 73, 94, 136-7
Tyne Turrets, 32, 58, 134-6

U-boat *U-27*, 97

Vickers 6-in gun of 1898, 22, 55
Volunteer Corps, 13, 79-84
Volunteer Special Service Sections, 24

Watkins, Colonel, 59
Wave Basin Battery, 21, 142
Wegener, Captain Lieutenant of U-27, 97
Wheatcroft Battery, 157
Whisky War, 88, 156
Whitburn Battery, 141
Whitby Battery, 157
Whitby, Bombardment, 97, 116-17
White, Lambert, Colonel, 27
Wireless sets, 67